D0507939

Mussolini and Italian Fascism

Hamish Macdonald

Historical Consultant:
Dr R. A. H. Robinson,
The University of Birmingham

040137

Stanley Thornes (Publishers) Ltd

First published in 1999 by:
Stanley Thornes (Publishers) Ltd,
Ellenborough House,
Wellington Street,
CHELTENHAM GL50 1YW
England

99 00 01 02 03 / 10 9 8 7 6 5 4 3 2 1

A catalogue record for this book is available from the British Library.

ISBN 0 7487 3386 8

Illustrated by Davide Provenzale, Angela Lumley (p.49)

Typeset by Tech-Set Ltd, Gateshead, Tyne and Wear

Printed and bound in Great Britain by Redwood Books, Trowbridge, Wiltshire

Acknowledgements

With thanks to the following for permission to reproduce copyright photographs in this book:

Centre for the Study of Cartoons and Caricature, University of Kent, Canterbury/ Evening Standard/ Solo Syndication, page 34; David King, page 43; Peter Newark, page 26; Moro Roma, pages 7, 15, 18, 23, 27, 29, 31 (col., bottom picture), 41 (col.) 45; *Punch* Magazine, pages 35, 38.

Every effort has been made to contact copyright holders. The publishers apologise to anyone whose rights have been inadvertently overlooked, and will be happy to rectify any errors or omissions.

To my students at Henbury School

Contents

How to Use this Book

History at A-level is a more complex and demanding subject than at any preceding level, and it is with these new and higher demands on students in mind that the Pathfinder History series has been written. The basic aim of the book is simple: to enable you to appreciate the important issues that underpin understanding of Mussolini's Fascist regime in Italy, how he rose to power and how he was toppled.

What this book does not do is provide a single source of answers needed for exam success. The very nature of A-level study demands that you use a range of resources in order to build up the understanding of different interpretations of issues, and in order to develop your own argument on exam topics. Pathfinder can make this subject more accessible by defining the Key Issues, giving an initial understanding of them and helping students to define questions for further investigation. It concentrates on the fundamentals surrounding Mussolini's impact on history; the important issues, events and other characters of his period that you must understand, and which the examiners will want to see that you know.

Pathfinder, therefore, becomes more of a guide book to the subject. It can be used whenever you want within the A-level course: as an introduction; as a reminder or revision text; or throughout the course each time a new topic is started. Pathfinder also has several important features to help you get to grips with Mussolini and his times.

The book follows the three basic stages of the A-level process, explaining why they are important and why you are doing them. The three sections of the book are thus Overview, Enquiry and Investigation, and Review. These describe the three main methods of studying history at A-level. Therefore, when, for example, you answer a question on the rise of Italian Fascism, you will recall why this book approaches this topic with these three headings in mind.

KEY ISSUES AND KEY SKILLS

Pathfinder is written around three basic principles. The first is that it covers the most important events, themes, ideas and concepts of the subject – the *Key Issues*. The second is that there are levels or tiers to these issues, so that a major question is broken down into its contributory questions and issues, making it easier to understand. Finally, there are fundamental skills that you must develop and employ as historians at this level – the *Key Skills*.

These three principles combine in Section 1, where **The Big Picture** sets the whole scene of the topic and identifies the most important periods and events within the topic. Then, **The Key Issues** establish what the author believes are the fundamental questions and answers to the subject as a whole, and examine these in more detail by raising contributory questions contained within the main question. (Each period is discussed in more detail in Section 2: you will see page references for the appropriate chapter in each case.) Each period, therefore, has its own issues and concepts, providing a second tier of Key Issues. Finally, **Information: Where to Find It and How to Use It** is a writing and researching section that offers hints and advice on the active study skills that you will be using in A-level history.

The main focus of the book is Section 2, called **Enquiry and Investigation** because this is exactly what you are being asked to do for most of the time during the A-level process. You are making historical enquiries and learning how to interpret sources and information every time you look at a document or analyse a photograph or read a topic. Each chapter takes as its title one of the periods identified in The Big Picture, and each one also identifies what you need to bear in mind when working on that particular issue or theme.

There is a useful little tab at the start of each double-page spread which summarises the most important aspects of the topic and identifies the skills that you will need to use when studying it. These are Key Skills, although you could think of them as key study skills if you prefer.

There are a number of Key Skills. They can be grouped together under the following headings with these definitions:

Skills for collecting information from historical sources

- Analysis: breaking down information into component parts (making notes under section headings, for example).
- Interpretation: considering the implications of information and cross-referencing to other sources or contextual knowledge in order to develop your understanding further. (Skills used within this are actually inference, deduction, extrapolation, interpolation, recall and synthesis.)
- Evaluation: assessing the validity of sources and the implications for the reliability of the information which they provide.
- Recording: arranging information into sections that allow easy retrieval when required; for example, making linear notes (good for large amounts of information), diagrams and flowcharts or mind maps (good for establishing relationships between sections of information).

Skills for applying and using information

- Explanation: using information to show how and why something happened.
- Assessment: weighing up possible explanations or interpretations.
- Forming hypotheses: setting up an explanation or judgement for further testing.
- Testing hypotheses: using information to support and challenge a hypothesis in order to improve it.
- Setting a thesis: using the information to present, support and sustain a tested hypothesis and explanation of historical processes.

Section 3: Testing a Hypothesis then brings all the interpretations, investigations and issues that you have looked at to do with Mussolini and Italian Fascism into one place. **Synthesis** is the bringing together of issues, arguments and judgements into overall answers. It also poses answers as to what the author considered to be the main issues identified in Section 1. **Argument** then takes the information and hypotheses and applies them to more detailed essay questions and answers – of the style that you might find, and that you might write, in the exam. **Review**, finally, is something of the author's own thoughts and conclusions on the subject at a broad level.

MARGINS AND ICONS

Pathfinder divides material as part of its strategy to focus attention on the most important issues. Therefore, the main central narrative discusses and interprets information but, although detailed, it cannot provide all of the information on its topic. It must be integrated and supplemented with more detailed works, articles and documents.

All other sorts of information appear in the margins and you will see the following icons used alongside them. Not all icons appear in every chapter, and some chapters have other features included as well, but the icons should help you to manage the extra information given on topics.

 Documents, historiography and sources – quotes from texts, individuals and passages

 Suggested headings for notes

 Suggested further reading

 Sample activities and exam-style questions

 General hints, study tips and advice

 Key words

Gaining an overview

After an introduction to the state of Italy around the time of the 1914–1918 war, this book gives a history of the rise and fall of Fascism in Italy between 1919 and 1945.

The purpose of this chapter is to give you an overview, The Big Picture. You can use it simply to help you to see the wood for the trees, or in the following ways:

- to pick up the gist of topics before closer study
- to focus your reading on the relevant things on which to make notes
- to give you a working knowledge of a topic to help prepare you for a lesson or lecture
- to review and gain a perspective on the whole period
- to revise

Major industrial area	Lands that Italians wanted to complete reunification

Milan • Venice • Trieste

Florence •

Corsica (France)

■ROME

Sardinia

Palermo

Areas of extreme poverty

Italy before the First World War 1870–1914 (see pages 12–13)

The Big Picture: Italy 1914–1945

ITALY AFTER THE FIRST WORLD WAR 1919 (SEE PAGES 14–15)

- Italy did not gain all that was hoped for from the peace settlements.
- A new system of elections by proportional representation produced weak governments which were unable to cope with inflation, high unemployment and strikes.

THE RISE OF FASCISM 1919–1922 (SEE PAGES 16–19)

- In 1919, Benito Mussolini launched the Fascist movement.
- 1918–1920 were the *bienno rosso* ('two red years'): Fascism became a mass movement by joining in a reaction against unrest caused by socialists in the towns and countryside.
- In 1921, Fascists gained respectability by helping Giolitti form a government.
- In 1922, Fascists violently seized power in the provinces from socialists.
- Fascists organised a 'March on Rome' and the king appointed Mussolini as Prime Minister.

FASCIST DICTATORSHIP 1922–1925 (SEE PAGES 20–23)

- In 1922, Mussolini created the Fascist Grand Council to 'advise' the government and made Fascist squads a part of a new legal 'Fascist Militia'.
- In 1923, a new electoral law gave the party that won a quarter of the votes two-thirds of the seats in the Chamber of Deputies; Mussolini forced Greece to pay compensation to Italy for the assassination of an Italian general on the island of Corfu.
- In 1924, Yugoslavia gave up Fiume to Italy; outrage caused by the murder of the socialist Matteotti threatened the survival of Mussolini's government.
- In 1925, under pressure from the Fascist *ras* (bosses), Mussolini became a dictator.

THE TOTALITARIAN STATE 1925–1935 (SEE PAGES 24–35)

- Mussolini used the term 'totalitarian' in 1925, to describe the extent of the control that he wanted.
- In 1926, he banned all other political parties and non-Fascist trades unions, and created 'corporations' to represent the interests of workers and employers.
- He created a Special Tribunal (1926) and a new political police, OVRA (1927) to crush all political opposition.
- In 1929, the Lateran Treaties ensured that the Roman Catholic Church tolerated Mussolini's dictatorship. However, tensions remained.
- The Fascist regime sought to make Fascism popular through youth and student organisations, the school curriculum, welfare agencies and an after-work leisure organisation (*Dopolavro*), and through the use of cinema and radio.
- Mussolini sought prestige for Italy by acting as a statesman in western Europe, while plotting to destabilise the Balkans and to gain influence in North Africa.
- In 1935, Italy invaded Abyssinia (now Ethiopia).

RELATIONS WITH GERMANY AND MUSSOLINI'S DOWNFALL 1935–1945 (SEE PAGES 32–45)

- Italy and Germany sent military aid to support Franco against the Republican government in the Spanish Civil War (1936–1939); in 1936 Mussolini described Italy's relationship with Germany as an 'axis', around which all European countries could collaborate.
- In 1937, Italy and Germany joined Japan in a pact against communism.
- In May 1939, Italy and Germany formed an alliance called the 'Pact of Steel'.
- Mussolini's decision to take Italy to war in June 1940 resulted in a series of defeats in Greece and Africa. After the allies invaded Sicily in 1943, the king dismissed Mussolini. However, the Germans rescued him from prison and made him head of a new Fascist state in northern Italy.
- The Resistance captured and killed Mussolini on 28 April 1945.

Benito Mussolini, 1883–1945
The son of a blacksmith and school mistress, Mussolini was a failure as a school teacher, but was a brilliant journalist. An ex-socialist, he founded the Fascist movement in Italy and was Il Duce (the leader). His declared aim was to make Italy 'great, respected and feared'.

Inflation – when prices rise, causing a fall in the value of money

Proportional representation – a system of election whereby the number of elected representatives (for example, MPs) for each party is decided by the proportion of votes that each party receives

Fascist – from the Italian, *fascio* (plural *fasci*), used in a political sense to mean a 'union' or 'league'

Totalitarian – exercising control over all aspects of life, with the interests of the state being put before those of the individual

The Key Issues

1. WHAT WAS THE IMPACT OF THE FIRST WORLD WAR?

The terms 'turning-point', 'watershed' and 'catalyst' are often used to describe the effects of the First World War on Italy. Why was Mussolini expelled from the Socialist Party? Were there others who believed that the war would bring about the national regeneration of Italy? Did the war act as a catalyst in bringing their ideas together? To what extent did the war create conditions that were ripe for the rise of Fascism? What economic and other burdens did the war place on Italy? To what extent was nationalist enthusiasm frustrated?

2. HOW DID MUSSOLINI COME TO POWER?

Within four years of forming the Italian Fascist movement, Mussolini became Prime Minister in 1922. To what extent did the failure of five successive governments to solve Italy's postwar problems, as well as the internal divisions within the two largest parties, the Catholic PPI and the Socialist PSI, allow Mussolini to take advantage of popular disillusionment? What lessons had Mussolini learned from D'Annunzio's coup in Fiume? How much did popular fears of a communist (Bolshevik) revolution help Mussolini's cause? How important was the support won from businessmen in the northern industrial cities, and from landowners, estate managers and farmers in the Po valley and Tuscany by the use of Fascist action squads to break up strikes and to destroy the power of the peasant leagues? What did the political skills of Mussolini contribute? How pivotal was the role of the king during the 'March on Rome' crisis of October 1922?

3. WHY DID MUSSOLINI BECOME A DICTATOR?

When did the transformation begin from coalition government to one-party dictatorship? Was the crisis resulting from the murder of the Socialist Deputy, Matteotti, the turning-point? Or did the process begin earlier, when the Fascists introduced a new electoral law in 1923? Did Mussolini become dictator just because he was put under pressure from the *ras*, the provincial Fascist leaders?

4. HOW COULD MUSSOLINI'S DICTATORSHIP BE DEFINED?

Was Mussolini's dictatorship more than just an authoritarian regime? Did it ever become truly 'fascistised'? To what extent was the reality a compromise with the Church, industrialists and the king? How much of an achievement were the Lateran Treaties of 1929? How far did the Pope collaborate with, rather than oppose, the Fascist regime – and why? Did the creation of corporations, joining both workers and employers together, end class conflict and give equal rights and obligations to both sides? What independent representation did trades unions and employers, respectively, retain? Why did the king not crush the Fascist uprising prior to the 1922 'March on Rome', or dismiss Mussolini after the 1924 Matteotti crisis? Why did he support Mussolini's dictatorship until 1943?

5. MUSSOLINI'S FOREIGN POLICY – OPPORTUNIST OR PLANNED?

Was Mussolini a showman on the look-out for opportunities to gain prestige for Italy in world affairs and to boost the popularity of his dictatorship? Did his foreign policy tend to be impulsive rather than rational and planned in advance? Or did Mussolini set out from the start to revise the peace settlements to Italy's advantage and make Italy the key to the balance of power in the Mediterranean, at the expense of Britain and France?

The invasion of Abyssinia in 1935 is generally accepted as a turning-point. To what extent was it the outcome of long-term imperial ambitions in Africa? Was it motivated by domestic concerns to keep up the momentum of support for Fascism? Was it influenced by the re-emergence of Germany as a rival power in Europe? The year 1935 also marked a watershed in relations with Germany. To what extent was the 'friendship' that developed between the two countries responsible for Mussolini's downfall?

6. WHAT DID MUSSOLINI ACHIEVE FOR ITALY?

Mussolini achieved a longer period of strong government and a greater degree of international status for the modern state of Italy than ever before. Other achievements included the reconciliation of Church and state, as well as major projects such as land reclamation in the Pontine Marshes. However, to what extent was the popularity and success of the Fascists disguised by censorship, media manipulation, propaganda and the banning of political opposition? Did Fascism heal the divisions between the rural south and the industrialised north? Did Fascism harmonise relations between workers and employers, or bring about a classless society? How progressive were Fascist policies towards women? How popular was the increasing German influence upon Italy? Would Mussolini have done better to have kept Italy out of the Second World War?

7. WHAT WAS ITALIAN FASCISM?

Can you dismiss Italian Fascism as a nationalist, violent and authoritarian movement in which style, propaganda and a negative attitude towards other ideologies were a substitute for a coherent and positive agenda? Evidence for this would be the improvised nature of Fascism and its inconsistencies; the abandonment of much of the Fascists' original programme of 1919; and the speedy collapse of the Fascist regime after the fall of Mussolini.

Or should the ideological roots of Fascism be taken more seriously, bearing in mind the re-emergence of Fascist movements in postwar Italy and in other European countries, and the fact that Fascism is seen to be older than the movement launched by Mussolini in 1919? It has been suggested that Italian Fascism was a search for a radical way forward to national regeneration, and an alternative to either liberalism or socialism. Does the evidence support this interpretation?

Defining history

Question: Why study 'Key Issues' rather than concentrating on the true story of what happened?

Answer: Reconstructing the story of the past is not straightforward. This is precisely why issues for discussion arise. At A-level it is important to understand more about the nature of history.

There are three ways of defining history:

1 History is what actually happened in the past, independent of the historian. This is very difficult to recover without some loss of evidence and distortion.

2 History is the activity of enquiry based on evidence. This requires the skills of a good detective.

3 History is what historians write about the past based upon their interpretation of evidence. Good historians are good storytellers too!

The word 'history' comes from a Classical Greek word, *historia*, meaning 'enquiry'.

Books and other sources of information

Popular histories – written for the general public, for light reading and entertainment; usually more narrative than analysis

General histories – syntheses of research on broad topics, written for non-specialists.

Specialist studies – original research on specific subjects or themes

Textbooks – written to support courses for different levels of study

Biographies, autobiographies, and published Memoirs and diaries

Periodicals – magazines of articles and book reviews

Theses – research (mostly unpublished) for academic qualifications such as a 'Masters' or 'doctoral' degree (e.g. MA or PhD)

Historical reference books – dictionaries of history or historical terms, chronologies and encyclopaedias (including CD-ROMs)

Primary sources – a range of official and unofficial written and pictorial evidence, including contemporary literature, maps, prints, paintings, political cartoons and photographs

Maps, pictures and novels

Maps are an essential tool. They give a sense of spatial relationships and distances; show political and natural boundaries and natural resources; give clues about climate and topography; and show how geography and environment help to shape decisions and strategy.

Political cartoons and photographs add a vital visual dimension to understanding, and also stimulate the imagination. Contemporary novels reflect attitudes, depict social relations and give a feel for the language and atmosphere of the period.

Information: Where to Find It and How to Use It

1. WHERE TO FIND INFORMATION

This book is designed as a 'pathfinder' to guide you through a history of Mussolini and Fascist Italy at A-level. The serious A-level student will use it as a starting-point or as a companion to the study of other sources of information. Examiners expect breadth and depth of reading. At first, this may seem a daunting prospect. However, there are short-cuts and skills to learn which can save you a lot of time, money and effort – and increase the pleasure of study. The first important short-cut is to be clear about what you are looking for and what different kinds of information there are to help you find it. This book will point you in the direction of relevant topic headings and, in the margins, will suggest books for further reading. However, as you will see in the margin of this chapter, there are several different types of history book.

A library is an obvious place to look for other sources of information. (Libraries are organised into different sections and not all books are stored on the open shelves. A lending library is for borrowing books and music; a reference library contains a huge range of sources for study in the library only.) First, use the catalogue system. Modern libraries have a very user-friendly computer that guides you through your search. Older libraries and reference libraries may still have a card index system. Many professionally run libraries use a method of referencing books called the Dewey system. In this system, books on the history of Italian Fascism start at 945.091. The computer or card index catalogue will give you this number to assist your search for the right section and shelf on which to find a particular book. The computer will also tell you if the book is out on loan or stored in a different place from the open shelves.

2. WHAT TO LOOK FOR WHEN CHOOSING A BOOK FOR A-LEVEL STUDY

Check that you can manage the language level. For basic facts, start with simple, easy-to-read texts; for example, books written for younger students or popular histories written for the general public. Use encyclopaedias (including those on CD-ROM) and other reference books, including dictionaries of history. Books specially written for A-level students avoid, or take the trouble to explain, difficult words and historical terms. However, a good student will not rely on them alone, as they may deliberately simplify complex issues and may not reflect up-to-date research. Check the date of publication to see how recent it is. Does the book have an index to help you find key topics quickly? Does it have a bibliography (a reading list) and references to sources used?

3. TIME MANAGEMENT

A key skill is to reduce time wasting. Work out how much time you have available and be ruthless with it. Plan ahead. Develop a routine for efficient study habits. Get into a rhythm of work, so that you improve study skills through regular practice. Allocate different lengths of time for different types of task, such as searching catalogues for reference numbers, previewing and selecting sources, and reading and making notes. Avoid 'pencil sharpening' – in other words, putting off the actual moment at which you get started. Time yourself. Do tasks which require most concentration and thinking (such as reading and making notes) first, and more mechanical tasks (such as writing up, checking and editing) second. Remember that there are no medals for unnecessary hours of labour. Take short-cuts.

4. ACTIVE READING

Few people read a history book all the way through without nodding off! It's not a novel. History books are meant to be 'gutted and filleted' like fish. Here is a possible scheme that you could use:

- have an idea of key questions or topics before you start reading
- use the index or chapter headings to find relevant sections of the book
- skim-read to locate the relevant information
- jot down possible subheadings
- re-read and confirm the heading titles – and try to make them memorable (a bit like brief newspaper headlines)
- for each subheading, look for no more than three key points to note
- use abbreviations to speed you up

5. MAKING NOTES

The purpose of making notes is to make a short-cut to information that you may need later, and to provide prompts and cues for your memory. There are different ways of making notes, each of which have their own advantages. Here are two examples:

- *The spider diagram.* This starts with a Key Issue or question in the centre, around which there is a web of headings, subheadings and key points. It has the advantage of being visually easy to take in at a glance and of showing connections.
- *Headings followed by numbered points.* Typically, a main heading is followed by subheadings under each of which key points (with useful names and important dates) are numbered – usually in twos and threes. The advantage of this system is that, for revision, a copy of the headings can be used to test knowledge and, under exam conditions, recall of relevant headings can trigger the necessary key points.

It is a good idea to leave a blank sheet between each page, or at the ends of sections of notes, for adding references to useful books, the occasional useful quotation, and additional notes picked up from lessons, further reading or during revision.

Breadth and depth

Question: What is meant by 'breadth' and 'depth' of reading?

Answer: 'Breadth' means reading a range of books to build up knowledge of context, and of different perspectives and interpretations. 'Depth' means analysis of evidence and reading for knowledge of detail.

Selected general histories: Roger Eatwell, *Fascism, a History* (Vintage, 1996); Roger Griffin, *The Nature of Fascism* (Routledge, 1991); Martin Clark, *Modern Italy 1871–1995* (Longman, 2nd edn, 1996); Alan Cassels, *Fascist Italy* (Routledge and Kegan Paul, 1969); Martin Blinkhorn, *Mussolini and Fascist Italy* (Methuen, 1984); John Whittam, *Fascist Italy* (Manchester University Press, 1995); Philip Morgan, *Italian Fascism, 1919–1945* (Macmillan, 1995); David Williamson, *Mussolini: from Socialist to Fascist* (Hodder and Stoughton, 1997); Alexander De Grand, *Italian Fascism: its Origins and Development* (University of Nebraska Press, 2nd edn, 1989).

Selected specialist histories: Esmonde M. Robertson, *Mussolini as Empire-builder: Europe and Africa 1932–36* (Macmillan, 1977); MacGregor Knox, *Mussolini Unleashed, 1939–1941* (Cambridge University Press, 1982); Robert Mallett, *The Italian Navy and Fascist Expansionism 1935–40* (Frank Cass, 1998).

Selected biographies: Denis Mack Smith, *Mussolini* (Granada, 1981); Jasper Ridley, *Mussolini* (Constable, 1997).

Selected novels: Ignazio Silone, *Fontamara* (1933); Giorgo Bassani, *The Garden of the Finzi-Continis* (Quartet, 1962).

THE KEY ISSUE

- What was Italy like before the First World War?

THE KEY SKILLS

Investigation

Analysis

WHAT YOU HAVE TO DO

Investigate and work out what the economic, social and political problems of Italy were like before the war.

Key

1 Piedmont
2 Liguria
3 Lombardi
4 Trentino—Alto-Adige
5 Emilia-Romagna
6 Veneto
7 Friuli
8 Tuscany
9 Umbria
10 Marches
11 Latium (Roma)
12 Sardinia
13 Abruzzi
14 Molise
15 Campania
16 Puglia
17 Basilicata
18 Calabria
19 Sicily

The regions of Italy

Obstacles to the *Risorgimento*: economic and social divisions; low levels of literacy; Vatican hostility; widespread lack of faith in politicians; lack of great power status.

Italy after Unification in 1870

RISORGIMENTO

In 1914, the population of Italy was 38 million. However, few Italians had a strong sense of national identity. The unification of Italy had come about between 1859 and 1870, largely as a result of the ambitions of one state, Piedmont. As the Piedmontese politician, D'Azeglio, put it, 'We have made Italy – now we must make Italians.' This process of nation-building, known as the *Risorgimento*, faced a number of obstacles.

ECONOMIC AND SOCIAL DIVISIONS

While 58% of Italians depended on agriculture for a living, only 23% depended on industry. There were huge economic divisions between northern and southern Italy. The harnessing of rivers to create hydroelectric power had made possible the rapid industrialisation of the north-west. New job opportunities led to rapidly expanding towns and cities, and the creation of a modern industrial working class. Industrialisation also created a powerful class of businessmen and bankers, and a new urban lower middle class.

Meanwhile, new farming methods and technology were introduced in the fertile Po Valley and areas such as Tuscany. These had not only transformed these regions from economic backwardness, but had also produced significant social changes. At the bottom was a large class of rural labourers, and then a layer of estate managers and technical experts who, in turn, looked up to a new rich farm-owning class known as the *agrari*. While the *agrari* prospered, poor farmers who rented their land and sharecroppers (peasants who gave up part of their crop to their landlords) found it harder to make a living.

While these developments had far-reaching effects upon northern and central Italy, the economy of the south remained very poor and backward. Advances in medicine had led to remedies for diseases such as malaria, and a reduction of epidemics such as cholera. This meant that it became possible to open up low-lying and previously almost uninhabitable countryside in southern and central Italy for farming. The rural population in areas such as Basilicata had almost doubled since 1870. Nevertheless, the gulf between the prosperous north and poverty-stricken southern Italy remained.

LACK OF FAITH IN THE RULING POLITICIANS

The new Italian state was the creation of liberal politicians who had faith in a parliamentary system and eventual democracy. By 1912, most Italian males had the right to vote. Few, however, saw any value in exercising their right, because the corrupt political system kept the same politicians in power. This practice was known as *trasformismo*.

THE HOSTILITY OF THE VATICAN

The Vatican (the headquarters of the Roman Catholic Church) had ruled a significant proportion of the Italian peninsula before 1861 and was opposed to the creation of an Italian state from the outset. In 1873, the government confiscated and redistributed £20 million worth of Church land. The Pope retaliated in 1874 by banning Catholics from taking part in politics. Although this ban was relaxed in 1904, tensions continued to exist between the new state of Italy and the Roman Catholic Church.

ITALIA IRREDENTE AND DREAMS OF EMPIRE

Italians who cared about the *Risorgimento* believed that the unification of Italy and nation-building were far from complete. The regions of Trentino and Trieste remained under Austrian rule, despite containing large numbers of Italian speakers. These were the so-called *terre irredente* (unredeemed lands) that patriotic Italians yearned to reclaim. This strained relations in the Triple Alliance, formed between Italy, Austria and Germany in 1882. Meanwhile, nationalists wanted an empire to rival those of Britain, France and the new Germany. However, Italy's efforts to expand its empire in Africa were frustrated by France's occupation of Tunis and British control of Egypt. Moreover, Italy suffered a humiliating setback in Abyssinia (now Ethiopia) at the battle of Adowa in 1896, in which more Italians died in one day than in all the battles of the *Risorgimento*.

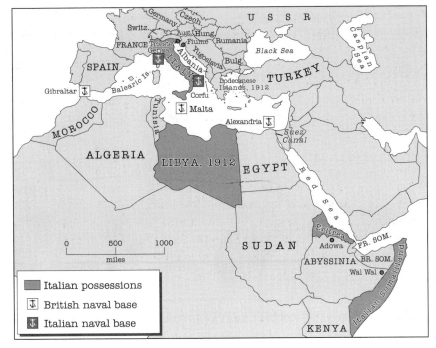

Italy's empire in 1914

Legend:
- Italian possessions
- British naval base
- Italian naval base

Illiteracy statistics across Italy (1911 Census)

Piedmont	11%
Tuscany	37%
Basilicata	59%
Calabria	70%
Sicily	58%

Although primary education had been declared compulsory in 1877, as many as 38% of Italians (70% in the south) could not read or write by 1914. Only about 7% of so-called Italians spoke Italian – most spoke a regional dialect.

Giovanni Giolitti, 1842–1928

Giolitti was the dominant liberal statesman before the Great War. Prime Minister three times between 1903 and 1914 (November 1903–March 1905, May 1906–December 1909 and March 1911–March 1914), he was a cynical, pragmatic politician, who tried to take the sting out of socialism with a number of mild social reforms that included extending the vote to almost all adult males in 1912. He became the focus of criticisms for the failures of Italian liberalism.

The state of the nation

Imagine being an Italian politician before the First World War, assessing with colleagues the state of the nation. In small groups, try to answer the following questions:

- What social, economic and political problems need to be overcome to complete the *Risorgimento*?
- What will be the likely effects on Italy and its people of a major war?

THE KEY ISSUE

- What was the impact of the war on Italy?

THE KEY SKILL

Assessment

WHAT YOU HAVE TO DO

Find out why Italy joined the war on the side of Britain and France in 1915, and which sections of the population benefited and which suffered as a result.

Mussolini's revolution ...

'We have already made a revolution. In May 1915 ... it overturned a shameful situation at home and decided the outcome of the World War.'

Benito Mussolini, on forming the Fascist movement in March 1919

See Martin Clark, *Modern Italy 1871–1995* (Longman, 2nd edn, 1996) and Martin Blinkhorn, *Mussolini and Fascist Italy* (Methuen, 1984).

Italy in 1919

WAR!

The outbreak of war divided Italians into those who wanted Italy to stay out of it and those who wanted to fight; in other words, neutralists and interventionists. The majority, which included most socialists, Catholics and liberals, were neutralists. They helped to create a myth that a noisy campaign by interventionists pushed Italy into the war in 1915. In fact, the key decisions were taken by the Prime Minister, Salandra, the Foreign Minister, Sonnino, and King Vittorio Emmanuele III. First, they attempted to bargain with Austria – their ally since 1882 – to restore Trentino and Trieste to Italy as a price for support, before striking a better deal with Britain, France and Russia in the Treaty of London (May 1915).

Parliament then gave its backing, after a month of street demonstrations organised by the interventionists, who formed revolutionary action groups called *Fasci di Azione Rivoluzionaria*. These groups were an odd mixture of rebels from all parties, including socialists such as Mussolini, revolutionary trades unionists, artists who called themselves 'futurists', radicals and republicans. However, they all had one thing in common. They saw the war as an opportunity for national regeneration: a purging of the old style of politics, the forging of a strong sense of national unity, and the creation of Italy as a world power.

THE IMPACT OF THE WAR

The war intensified divisions within Italy. It gave a dramatic boost to the industries that it most affected: steel, engineering, vehicles, cement, hydroelectric power, chemicals, rubber and woollen textiles. Rapid expansion to meet demands for armaments and vehicles was concentrated in the north, requiring more industrial workers. Harsh, military discipline in the factories did not prevent the growth of trades unions and strikes. Firms such as Breda, Fiat and Pirelli made huge profits and became famous throughout Europe; but their levels of production could not be maintained in peacetime.

Five million men were called up to fight. Casualties were high. At least 600 000 died, and 1 million were wounded, of whom 450 000 were permanently disabled. The strain and exhaustion of war, and the rationing of food, go a long way to explaining why almost as many Italians died in the influenza epidemic of 1918–1919 as were killed in the whole 1914–1918 war.

To pay for the war, the government borrowed money and printed more bank notes. The national debt increased from 16 billion to 85 billion lire. As shortages of food and raw materials worsened, average shop prices quadrupled. Unemployment rose steeply at a time when 2.5 million men were released from the army. Over half were peasants or farm workers, whose expectations were raised by government pledges of land reform during the last years of the war. These promises were made to distract the soldiers from the propaganda of the Russian Bolsheviks, who were urging all workers to join the international revolution that they had started in 1917.

THE 'MUTILATED VICTORY'

Italy's Prime Minister, Orlando, and his Foreign Minister, Sonnino, went to the Paris Peace Conference to demand the full terms of the Treaty of London. They wanted Trentino, the South Tyrol as far as the Brenner Pass, Istria and Northern Dalmatia to be ceded to Italy. These were the conditions on which Italy had agreed to join the war on the side of Britain and France. In addition, they asked for the former Hungarian port of Fiume (Rijeka), on the grounds that most of the citizens in the centre of the town were Italians. Italy also expected to gain a share of the ex-German colonial territories in Africa.

Italy got most of what it wanted, except for Dalmatia, Fiume and the ex-German colonies. On balance, Italy had not done too badly. Its historic rival, Austria–Hungary, had been destroyed, and Italy now dominated the Adriatic Sea. But the refusal of the American President, Woodrow Wilson, to transfer Dalmatia and Fiume to Italy was felt to be very a public humiliation. Orlando and Sonnino had bungled the negotiations and fell from power. The result was what the popular nationalist, poet and war veteran, Gabriele D'Annunzio, called a 'mutilated victory'.

D'Annunzio then exposed the feebleness of the new Prime Minister, Francesco Saverio Nitti, by leading a military takeover of Fiume in September 1919. Top army officers supported him, together with a mixture of ex-servicemen, futurists, nationalists, syndicalists and adventurers. In defiance of the government, he held the city for 15 months; and demonstrated a new style of government, in which the economy would be run by ten corporations, which would elect the upper house of Parliament. Many of his ideas – including the setting up of a private army (militia), the use of the Roman salute, parades, speeches from balconies, the war cry, 'Eia, eia, alalà', and forcing opponents to swallow castor oil – were later adopted by the Fascist movement set up by Benito Mussolini.

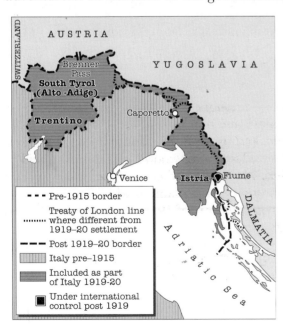

What Italy gained and did not gain from the 1919 peace settlement

- - - Pre-1915 border
······ Treaty of London line where different from 1919–20 settlement
- - - Post 1919–20 border
▨ Italy pre–1915
▨ Included as part of Italy 1919-20
■ Under international control post 1919

Gabriele D'Annunzio, 1863–1938
D'Annunzio earned a reputation before the war as a controversial poet, novelist and first socialist, then nationalist, politician. He campaigned for Italy's entry into the war in 1915 and became a war hero, being decorated many times for bravery. His popularity reached a peak at the end of the war, when he led an occupation of the port of Fiume in 1919. When he was eventually forced out, he retired to his villa at Gardone Riviera. He planned a march on Rome, but Mussolini beat him to it. In 1922, he gave an influential speech in Milan, supporting Fascism. In 1937, Mussolini called him the greatest living writer.

The occupation of Fiume

What factors contributed to Gabriele D'Annunzio leading an occupation of the port of Fiume? Why did this action win popular approval?

THE KEY ISSUES

- Why did Fascism attract little support in 1919?
- How did Fascism become a mass movement?

THE KEY SKILLS

Analysis of evidence and causes
Reconciling conflicting evidence

WHAT YOU HAVE TO DO

Discover how the nature of Fascism developed after the failure of the Fascists in the elections of 1919.

The Futurist Manifesto

'We intend to sing the love of danger, the habit of energy and fearlessness.

Courage, audacity and revolt will be the essential ingredients of our poetry.

We will glorify war – the world's only hygiene ...

We will sing of great crowds excited by work, by pleasure, and by riot ...'

From the Futurist Manifesto by Filippo Marinetti, writing in Le Figaro, 1909

Arditi – First World War shock troops, known as 'the daring ones'

Syndicalist – a revolutionary trade unionist

Vanguard – the group leading the army's front line; activists who lead the way

The Search for a Third Way

MUSSOLINI'S SOCIALIST ROOTS

Benito Mussolini was born near Forlì in the Romagna. His mother was a schoolteacher, and his father a blacksmith and fiercely socialist. He had attempted teaching without success, before drifting into politics and journalism. Before the war, he gained a reputation as a revolutionary socialist. On 9 January 1910, he wrote, 'Socialist workers must form the vanguard, vigilant and combative, that spurs the mass never to forget the vision of the ideal goal.'

He became the editor of the socialist newspaper, *Avanti!*, in 1912. However, his support for the campaign to join the war caused him to part company with the Socialist Party and set up his own newspaper, *Il Popolo d'Italia*, with money from business and French sources. He joined the army and served with enthusiasm, until injured when a grenade-thrower blew up during a training exercise. Unable to fight as a soldier, he returned to journalism and politics.

A POLITICAL MOVEMENT

At a meeting in Milan on 23 March 1919, attended by 118 people, the 36-year-old Mussolini launched the *Fascio di Combattimento* (Combat Group). The root cause of this move was a frustration with party politics. The term *fascio* (plural *fasci*), which in a political sense means 'union' or 'group', had been used before by revolutionary syndicalists, who set up the *Fascio di Azione Rivoluzionaria* to rally support for Italy's entry into the war. The intention was to find an alternative third way in politics, which would appeal to those who had fought for their country and bring together nationalists and socialists. Among those who attended this first meeting were an assortment of disgruntled ex-servicemen, syndicalists and radicals from various parties. Also present was the artist, Filippo Marinetti, the author of the *Futurist Manifesto* (1909). The Fascist political programme agreed was extremely radical.

> The resulting *Fascists' Programme* of 6 June 1919 stated:
> 'We require:
> – *Scrutin de liste* (universal suffrage with a system of regional voting for a list of parties rather than candidates), proportional representation, with votes for women and their eligibility for office.
> – Minimum age for votes lowered to 18; that for deputies lowered to 25.
> – Abolition of the Senate.
> – A foreign policy aimed at enhancing Italy's position in the world through peaceful competition among the civilised nations.
> – A heavy, extraordinary and progressive taxation on capital which would involve a meaningful partial expropriation of all forms of wealth.
> – The confiscation of all property belonging to religious organisations.'

However, in the first elections using the new rules of proportional representation, held in November 1919, each local Fascist group decided its own electoral programme. They did not win enough votes for a single Fascist candidate to be elected. Mussolini thought seriously about emigrating to America. The two mass parties to emerge were the socialists (PSI) and the Catholic *Popolari* (PPI).

THE SHADOW OF D'ANNUNZIO

During 1919, the war hero and nationalist poet, Gabriele D'Annunzio, easily overshadowed Mussolini. His theatrical 15-month occupation of the Adriatic port of Fiume, in defiance of the peace-makers and of the Italian government, grabbed the headlines. He was only forced out in 1920 by Prime Minister Giolitti's unpopular decision to send in the army. The demise of D'Annunzio gave Mussolini the opportunity to step into the spotlight that he had vacated. The Fascists attracted many of D'Annunzio's supporters to their organisation, having in common the Roman salute, the uniform of black shirts of the *arditi*, the staging of elaborate ceremonies and the making of balcony speeches.

THE *BIENNIO ROSSO* 1919–1920

During the *biennio rosso* ('two red years') of 1919–1920, a wave of strikes and land occupations, organised by trades unions and peasant leagues, gripped Italy. Encouraged by socialists and left-wing *Popolari*, workers occupied factories and peasants took over plots of land. In many areas, socialists took control of local government and intimidated any workers and peasants who were unwilling to join their unions or leagues. However, the reaction of the Giolitti government infuriated and humiliated employers. He put pressure on them to make concessions to the strikers. Mussolini seized this opportunity to send in *squadre d'azione* (action squads) to assist businessmen in the northern industrial cities and landowners, estate managers and farmers in the Po valley and Tuscany by breaking up strikes in factories and by destroying the power of the peasant leagues in the countryside.

SQUADRISTI VIOLENCE

The *squadristi* also proved to be highly effective security guards for frightened businessmen and bankers, who rewarded their services with money for Fascist funds. This alliance with employers upset a number of 'Fascists of the first hour', such as Marinetti and the syndicalists, but transformed Fascism into a mass movement in northern and central Italy. Commanded by local Fascist leaders known as *ras* (an Abyssinian/Ethiopian word for chieftain), the action squads sacked and burnt down the offices and newspaper printing shops of the Socialist Party, trades unions and Catholic peasant leagues. Typically, they beat up opponents with clubs (called *manganelli*; singular *manganello*). They humiliated their victims by forcing them to drink castor oil or swallow live toads; or left them naked and tied up to trees, some distance from their homes. To this, the police and prefects – frequently targets of abuse by the socialists – more often than not turned a blind eye. Sometimes they even lent the squads vehicles with which to carry out their raids.

The squadristi

Source 1

'In the Po valley, the towns were on the whole less red than the country, being full of landowners, garrison officers, university students, rentiers, professional men, and trades people. These were the classes from which Fascism drew its recruits and which offered the first armed squads.'

Angelo Tasca, The Rise of Italian Fascism (Tasca was expelled from the Italian Communist Party in 1929)

Source 2

'Besides, we knew those men in black shirts ... if we looked at them straight in the eye they looked away. They too were poor men of a special kind, landless, jobless – or with many jobs, which is the same thing – and averse to hard work. Too weak and cowardly to rebel against the rich and the authorities, they preferred serving them in order to be able to rob other poor men, *cafoni* [peasants], smallholders.'

Ignazio Silone, Fontamara (Silone wrote this novel in 1930 after he, too, was expelled from the Italian Communist Party)

What problems do sources 1 and 2 present to historians studying the membership of the *squadristi*?

THE KEY ISSUES

- How important was the role of Mussolini in the Fascists' route to power?
- How important was the role of King Vittorio Emmanuele in the Fascists' rise to power?

THE KEY SKILLS

Assessment
Understanding, analysis and interpretation of causes

WHAT YOU HAVE TO DO

Decide how much personal credit Mussolini deserves for assisting the rise of Fascism, compared with the *ras* and his political rivals.

The Fascist programme

Prepare a presentation lasting no more than five minutes which answers the following questions:

- How much of the Fascists' original programme did Mussolini abandon?
- Why was there tension between Mussolini and the *ras*?

Five Blackshirts from a Fascist Action Squad, armed with manganelli *(truncheons)*

The Route to Power

FROM MOVEMENT TO PARTY

Mussolini presented Fascism as a stabilising influence that could restore law and order, and hinted at the possibility of tactical alliances with senior politicians. Giolitti invited the Fascists to campaign in the election of May 1921 as part of his anti-socialist National Bloc, with a view to forming a coalition government. The Fascists won 35 seats and gained instant respectability – whereupon Mussolini denounced any arrangement with Giolitti. However, by the summer of 1921 Mussolini was worried that increasing *squadristi* violence would give the divided opposition cause to unite against the Fascists. Moreover, on 31 July at Sarzana, 12 *carabinieri* easily routed 500 Fascists.

Therefore, on 2 August, he signed a peace pact with moderate socialists and the General Confederation of Workers (CGL), the main trade union body. This provoked a serious clash with the *ras*, who were powerful enough locally to challenge Mussolini. However, judging that no single one of them was powerful enough to replace him as *Duce*, Mussolini resigned from the Fascist Central Committee – and used the ensuing leadership crisis to his advantage. At a Fascist National Congress held in November, a compromise was reached: the Fascist movement became the National Fascist Party, with Mussolini as leader. In return, all local *fasci* were to form squads, and the pact with the socialists was dropped. The creation of a central party organisation gave Mussolini more authority over the *ras* and allowed him to abandon most of what remained of the original 1919 Fascist programme, including hostility to the Catholic Church. This was particularly important, because the new Pope, Pius XI (who as Archbishop of Milan had blessed the Fascists' banners), did not support the Catholic *Popolari* leader, Sturzo.

REVOLUTION AND INTRIGUE

Over the next few months, the Fascists carried out an effective revolution in the northern and central provinces of Italy. In May 1922, Balbo led 50 000 of the unemployed into Ferrara and blackmailed the government into funding an ambitious public works programme as the price for ending the occupation. At Bologna, the government gave in to Fascist demands to remove an unfriendly prefect. In July, Fascists took control of Cremona, Rimini and Ravenna. A socialist attempt to rally resistance by calling for a general strike on 31 July played into the hands of the Fascists – they helped to break up the strike by 3 August and then took over Ancona, Livorno and Genoa.

While opposition remained hopelessly divided, Mussolini maintained contact with ex-Prime Ministers Salandra, Orlando, Nitti and Giolitti, having them believe he might join one of them in a coalition government. In September 1922, he declared that he was no longer anti-monarchist and that the Fascists were well disposed towards the army.

THE PLAN TO MARCH ON ROME

By October 1922, the Fascists occupied Trento and Bolzano. Mussolini then foiled a plan by Prime Minister Facta to win the support of Giovanni Giulietti, a powerful syndicalist leader based in Genoa, and his ally D'Annunzio, by disbanding the Fascist Union in Genoa and allowing Giulietti's seamen's union to represent the sailors in negotiations with the shipowners.

On 24 October, Fascist *squadristi* from all over southern Italy converged on Naples to hear Mussolini. He told them: 'Either we are allowed to govern or we will seize power by marching on Rome.' A careful plan was formed. Four *ras* – Balbo, Bianchi, Cesare De Vecchi and General De Bono – were to coordinate the takeover of public buildings and key sites in the main cities before a March on Rome on 27–28 October. Resisting pressure to resign, Prime Minister Facta prepared to use the army to defend Rome against the Fascists. For this, he needed final approval from King Vittorio Emmanuele.

While waiting for the royal signature, the army went into action to crush the revolt outside Rome. They met with little resistance from the Fascists and easily reoccupied buildings taken overnight. To prevent the Fascists from reaching Rome, roads and railways were blocked. Cesare De Vecchi made it clear that he would obey the king if given a choice. There was talk among senior Fascists of killing Mussolini if necessary. In Milan, the prefect, Alfredo Lusignoli, received instructions to arrest Mussolini. The Fascists bribed him to ignore his orders, with the offer of a seat in the Cabinet. His failure to act was, according to the historian Denis Mack Smith, 'a crucial factor in the success of the rebellion'.

THE ROLE OF THE KING

However, the king was pivotal in the Fascists' rise to power. At the last moment, he refused to back Facta and did not sign the decree to declare a state of emergency and impose martial law. Why did the king do this? Perhaps he feared putting the army's loyalty to the test and was worried about a possible palace coup by his pro-Fascist cousin, the Duke of Aosta. Leading politicians, industrialists, landowners, newspaper editors and clergy favoured accommodation rather than confrontation.

Facta resigned. The king called on Antonio Salandra to form a government. Salandra offered the Fascists four Cabinet posts in a coalition. Mussolini refused advice from De Vecchi and others to accept the offer. Salandra then advised the king to invite Mussolini to form a government instead. On 29 October 1922, at the age of 39, Mussolini became Prime Minister. On the next day, the king and the commanders of the army and navy saluted 70 000 Blackshirts as they marched through Rome to celebrate.

Carabinieri – local military police

Ras – the best known of the provincial Fascist leaders were **Italo Balbo** in Ferrara, **Roberto Farinacci** in Cremona, and **Dino Grandi** in Bologna

See Chapter 3 of Roger Eatwell, *Fascism, a History* (Vintage, 1996), Chapter 2 of John Whittam, *Fascist Italy* (Manchester University Press, 1995) and Chapters 4 and 5 of Denis Mack Smith, *Mussolini* (Granada, 1981).

Mussolini's background; 1919 Fascist movement formed – political programme; futurist ideas; early failures; D'Annunzio; *biennio rosso* ('two red years'); *ras* (local leaders); *squadrismo*; Fascism becomes a mass movement; Mussolini's leadership; formation of National Fascist Party (1921); divided and weak opposition; revolution in the provinces; March on Rome in October 1922; the role of the king.

For discussion and debate

Discuss the view that the Fascists would not have come to power in 1922 without the use of violence.

Towards Dictatorship

INTIMIDATION OF THE OPPOSITION

Mussolini's position as Prime Minister in October 1922 was by no means secure. The king had it in his power to dismiss Mussolini at any time should his coalition partners resign, and should opposition to the Fascists in Parliament unite sufficiently to offer an alternative government.

From the start, Mussolini intimidated his opponents and rivals. In his first speech to Parliament as Prime Minister on 16 November 1922, he claimed that with 300 000 armed Blackshirts behind him he could have formed an exclusively Fascist government had he wanted to. Both chambers of Parliament responded to this veiled threat by giving the new government votes of confidence. Five ex-Prime Ministers, including Giolitti and Facta, were among those who voted in favour. Shortly afterwards, Parliament granted the new government emergency powers for economic and administrative reforms.

SUPPORT FOR STRONG GOVERNMENT

Conservatives and liberals inside Parliament, and industrialists and landowners outside, wanted strong government after the political instability of the *biennio rosso*. They seemed reassured by the absence of socialists in Mussolini's first Cabinet, even though he would have liked to have included a socialist trade unionist in what he called a 'National Government'.

The appointment of Alberto De Stefani as Finance Minister strengthened the impression of normality and moderation rather than radical change. De Stefani was a liberal. His economic policies of reducing controls on industry, cutting taxes and freeing restrictions on trade led to less unemployment and a rapid increase in production. These policies greatly irritated many Fascists, who looked forward to radical economic policies and a social revolution. On the other hand, the air of respectability of the new government won the approval of people who could influence opinion outside Italy, such as the world-famous Italian philosopher, Benedetto Croce.

In December, Mussolini set up the Fascist Grand Council to work alongside the government Council of Ministers, which included ten non-Fascists. Mussolini himself was not only Prime Minister, but also Interior and Foreign Minister. The important decisions were taken at meetings of the Fascist Grand Council, which only the Fascist ministers could attend, and then officially approved by the Council of Ministers. The first decision taken was to create the Fascist Militia. This gave the Fascist Party a legally armed organisation that swore an oath of loyalty to Mussolini but not to the king, and which was paid for out of public funds.

THE KEY ISSUE

- Was Mussolini's government developing into a dictatorship before 1924?

THE KEY SKILLS

Analysis of evidence
Use of evidence and interpretation

WHAT YOU HAVE TO DO

Discover clues about Mussolini's intentions in government.

Mussolini's Cabinet

In his first Cabinet there were four Fascists, four liberals, two *Popolari* and one Nationalist. In Parliament, the 35 Fascist Deputies elected in May 1921 represented only 7% of the total. The Socialist Party had the largest group of Deputies (122), followed by the Catholic *Popolari* (107).

Future plans

'I could have abused my victory, but I refused to do so ... With 300 000 youths armed to the teeth, fully determined and almost mystically ready to act on any command of mine, I could have punished all those who defamed and tried to sully Fascism. I could have transformed this drab, silent hall into a bivouac for my squads ... [*loud applause from the right*] I could have barred the doors of Parliament and formed a government exclusively of Fascists ... but I chose not to for the present ...'

Benito Mussolini, speaking to the Chamber of Deputies on 16 November 1922

What hints does Mussolini give here about his future plans for power?

DEALING WITH THE OPPOSITION

Although Mussolini put De Bono, one of the leading *ras*, in charge of the police, he personally was in control. Over the next few months, he arrested several thousand political opponents. Mussolini followed a double policy. While secretly supporting illegal and often violent methods, publicly he gave reassurances that his approach was to bring about change peacefully. This was necessary because Mussolini depended on the *ras* and *squadristi*, as much as on good relations with the Church and with business, to keep him in power .

In March 1923, a small but significant rival party, the Nationalists, merged with the Fascists. Mussolini welcomed them because of their close links with big business and the army. They brought with them not only their own private army (the Blueshirts) but also key personalities such as Enrico Corradini, Luigi Federzoni and Alfredo Rocco, whose ideas influenced the future development of Fascism. In particular, they wanted a strong authoritarian government and a large Italian empire. Instead of class conflict, they sought a disciplined nation run by technically competent professionals committed to national competition. The Nationalists brought with them a conservative and disciplining influence, which caused ripples of resentment among the wilder and more radical elements of the Fascist movement.

The addition of Nationalist Deputies increased the number of Fascists in Parliament to 47 – hardly impressive in a chamber of 535. However, it meant that in any future election the inclusion of Nationalists on the Fascist list of approved candidates would attract more votes, especially in the south and the islands.

ELECTORAL REFORM

Mussolini was determined to strengthen the position of the Fascists in Parliament to make the legal basis of his government more secure. To do this, he ordered his Under-Secretary of State, Giacomo Acerbo, to prepare a new electoral law which would give any party or alliance two-thirds of the seats in Parliament if they won 25% of the votes. To make sure that this law was passed, despite being vastly outnumbered by opposition Deputies, Mussolini used the threat of the abolition of Parliament. Giolitti, Orlando and Salandra advised their followers to co-operate. During the debate, armed Fascists guarded the doors, while in the public galleries militia men made a show of fingering their daggers and revolvers. Parliament passed the law by a large majority.

THE POPE'S ASSISTANCE

Meanwhile, between April and June 1923, Mussolini involved Pope Pius XI in weakening the opposition of the Italian (or Catholic) People's Party (PPI). In April, he sacked the PPI ministers from his government because they refused to give him their unconditional support. Fearing that violence and intimidation were now being aimed at the clergy and the Church, Pius XI, a Fascist sympathiser, became involved. In June, he made the leader of the PPI, Luigi Sturzo, resign. During the passing of the Acerbo Law, most PPI Deputies abstained.

A marriage of convenience

Mussolini's private view of the merger between the Fascist and Nationalist parties was that it was 'a marriage of convenience and a purely tactical move for reasons of internal politics'.

See Alan Cassels, *Fascist Italy* (Routledge and Kegan Paul, 1969), Denis Mack Smith, *Mussolini* (Granada, 1981) and Philip Morgan, *Italian Fascism 1919–1945* (Macmillan, 1995).

Intentions of dictatorship ?

'Despite the fact that he temporarily observed existing constitutional forms, Mussolini was intent on becoming a dictator.'

Denis Mack Smith,
Mussolini, 1981

Find out if there is conclusive evidence to support this claim.

The Matteotti Crisis

SECRET TERROR AND NEW ALLIES

In January 1924, Mussolini ordered the setting up of a secret *cheka*, a ruthless squad of professional gangsters, to terrorise anti-Fascist troublemakers inside and outside Italy. Its leader, Amerigo Dumini, had an office in the Interior Ministry. A violent criminal, Dumini had proved in 1922 at Carrara that he could act without fear of arrest. There he had slapped a girl for wearing a red carnation – and then shot her mother and brother dead when they remonstrated with him.

Before the elections in April 1924 which followed the passing of the Acerbo Law, each party drew up electoral lists of approved candidates. Mussolini's list included non-Fascists who were nonetheless government supporters. Among these were two former Prime Ministers, Salandra and Orlando, conservative Catholics and liberals. Of the 3000 people who applied to be on the Fascist list, Mussolini chose 200 Fascists and 150 from other parties. Clearly, many non-Fascists saw support for Mussolini as an easy route to re-election.

CORRUPTION, VIOLENCE AND MURDER

Throughout the election campaign, politicians opposed to violence suffered harassment and physical intimidation. Mussolini personally ordered the prefects to disrupt opposition meetings where the government was criticised. Fascists prevented the liberal, Giovanni Amendola, from holding meetings and harassed the socialist leader, Giacomo Matteotti. A delighted Mussolini ordered that Dumini be given a bonus payment after his gang beat up opponents in broad daylight. Fascist thugs killed hundreds of people, including one socialist candidate. During the elections they confiscated voting certificates from their opponents and used them many times over. In several places, they even took the ballot boxes away before the count. It was not surprising that the Fascist-led coalition won 65% of the vote, giving them 374 seats out of 535 in the new Parliament.

With considerable courage, the socialist leader, Matteotti, stood up in Parliament on 30 May and made an angry speech, in which he listed examples of Fascist violence, intimidation and corruption during the election. He rejected the results as a fraud. On 10 June, as he was walking along the banks of the Tiber in Rome, Matteotti was seen being bundled into a car, which then sped off. A few hours later, Dumini is said to have brought Mussolini a piece of bloodstained upholstery from the car. Matteotti had apparently been stabbed to death. On the next day, despite the witnesses to Matteotti's kidnap, Mussolini publicly denied any knowledge of what had happened to him. However, this did not prevent a wave of revulsion throughout Italy which, for a time, threatened to bring down Mussolini's government. He suspended parliamentary proceedings in order to delay debate, put the Fascist Militia on alert, and ordered the arrest of Dumini and his gang.

THE KEY ISSUE

● Was the Matteotti crisis a turning-point in the development of the Fascist regime?

THE KEY SKILL

Interpretation

WHAT YOU HAVE TO DO

Important events are often seen from different points of view. Use the Key Skill to answer the Key Issue.

Interpretations of the crisis ...

Here are three different interpretations, from three historians, of the importance of the Matteotti crisis.

Source 1

'It has been well said that the Matteotti affair set in motion the conversion of a government into a regime.'

**Alan Cassels,
Fascist Italy, 1969**

Source 2

'The Matteotti crisis proved crucial to the development of a Fascist regime.'

**Martin Blinkhorn, Mussolini
and Fascist Italy, 1984**

Source 3

'The political crisis caused by the abduction and murder of the reformist Socialist Deputy Matteotti in June 1924 was not such a clear watershed between the periods of liberal democracy and Fascist systems of government.'

**Philip Morgan,
Italian Fascism, 1919–45, 1995**

Decide (i) what is different about the three interpretations, (ii) which is the most convincing and (iii) why.

THE AVENTINE SECESSION

Most of the opposition Deputies, led by the liberal, Giovanni Amendola, decided to boycott Parliament in protest. Their action came to be called the 'Aventine Secession', because it reminded people of a similar protest during the times of the ancient Roman Republic, when followers of Gaius Gracchus had taken to the Aventine Hill. This was a tactical error. The king, who was unwilling to accept their demands that he sack Mussolini anyway, used their 'unconstitutional behaviour' as an excuse. The Pope also came to Mussolini's rescue, by dissociating himself from the *Popolari* deputies who had joined the Aventine Secession. Further support came from leading industrialists, and even from the liberal philosopher, Croce.

The discovery of Matteotti's body in August (with, it is said, the knife still sticking in his chest) ensured that the pressure on Mussolini to resign continued. But when the king received a report containing more damning evidence of Fascist torture and murder, a group of leading *ras* visited Mussolini and threatened to overthrow him as their leader if he allowed the allegations to be investigated. They made it clear that they wanted Mussolini to set up a full dictatorship as the price for their continued support.

DICTATORSHIP

On 3 January 1925, Mussolini appeared to bow to the pressure from the *ras*. In a speech to the Chamber of Deputies, he took responsibility for what had happened (see margin). In the months that followed, a personal dictatorship took shape. It was spearheaded by the appointment of Roberto Farinacci as Party Secretary in February. He justified his reputation as one of the most ruthless of the *ras* by unleashing a wave of *squadristi* violence against all leading opponents of Fascism and by purging the party of any members who showed signs of disloyalty. In July, he imposed censorship. One by one, opposition leaders were picked off. Amendola died of injuries received in July following the worst of several assaults. Others, such as Filippo Turati, fled into exile.

On 3 August 1925, Mussolini banned meetings by all opposition parties. Democratically elected mayors of towns and cities were replaced by Fascist officials called *podestà*. An attempt to assassinate Mussolini by the socialist, Tito Zaniboni, on 4 November then led to a law which gave Mussolini almost unlimited power: On 24 December, he became Head of Government. This meant that he no longer needed Parliament and was accountable only to the king. However, few people knew that during 1925 he had fallen seriously ill. He had been receiving treatment for venereal disease for some years, but in February he was discovered to have a severe gastro-duodenal ulcer. Despite outward appearances and propaganda to the contrary, he was to remain in poor health. Nevertheless, Mussolini was now dictator of Italy.

Mussolini assumes responsibility

'I and I alone assume the political, moral, and historical responsibility for everything that has happened. If misquoted words are enough to hang a man, then out with the noose and gallows! If Fascism has been castor oil and club and is not a proud passion of the best of Italian youth, the blame is on me. If Fascism has been a criminal plot, if violence has resulted from a certain historical, political and moral atmosphere, the responsibility is mine, because I have deliberately created this atmosphere. Italy wants peace and quiet, work and calm. I will give these things with love if possible and with force if necessary.'

**Benito Mussolini,
3 January 1925**

Why do you think Mussolini survived in power after making the above speech?

Giacomo Matteotti

THE KEY ISSUE

- Did Mussolini create more than just an authoritarian regime between 1925 and 1928?

THE KEY SKILL

Interpretation

WHAT YOU HAVE TO DO

Find evidence to support Martin Clark's view that, 'Between 3 January 1925 and December 1928 the Italian State had been transformed. It had not been "fascistised."'

See Chapter 11 of Martin Clark, *Modern Italy 1871–1995* (Longman, 2nd edn, 1984) and Chapter 3 of Philip Morgan, *Italian Fascism, 1919–1945* (Macmillan, 1995).

Controlling the ministries

One reason why government ministries did not become more Fascist was that by 1929 Mussolini ran eight of them himself, including those of the armed forces. Since it was impossible for one person to carry out the duties of eight ministers, he delegated the detailed work to under-secretaries and civil servants.

Podestà – although party members, few *podestà* were Fascists: typically, they were conservative, elderly gentlemen who were local landowners, aristocrats or retired army officers; in practice, they prevented the real Fascists from taking over local government and helped the prefects to suppress *squadrismo*

Not a Fully Fascist Regime

LAW AND ORDER

In 1925, Mussolini made it clear that Fascist government would be 'totalitarian', summed up in the slogan: 'Everything within the State. Nothing outside the State. Nothing against the State.' It was expected that everything would be 'fascistised'; in other words, all positions of authority would be taken over by Fascists. In practice, Mussolini created an authoritarian regime that was not fully Fascist and that weakened the Fascist Party's influence.

Mussolini relied on the police, the courts, the civil service and the army to maintain law and order. Most senior positions remained in traditional hands rather than being given to Fascists as a reward for their loyal service. The Interior Minister, Luigi Federzoni, and the Minister of Justice, Alfredo Rocco, were conservatives and ex-Nationalists. The Chief of Police from 1926 to 1940, Arturo Bocchini, and his successor, were career prefects. In 1943, of 117 prefects in office, only 37 were political appointments. Civil servants joined the Fascist Party to keep their jobs.

Unlike Nazi Germany, there was no SS or *Gestapo*. Mussolini first referred to an organisation called 'OVRA' in 1930. Assumed to be a new secret police, OVRA was, in fact, an extension of the traditional secret branch of the Interior Ministry, using a wider network of informers. The prefects, top civil servants who governed the provinces, organised the police, were responsible for law and order, and appointed the *podestà* who, in 1926, replaced elected mayors and local councils.

THE TAMING OF THE PARTY

Farinacci's appointment as Party Secretary proved to be a shrewd choice. One of the most extreme of the *ras*, Farinacci set about purging the party of disloyal elements and unleashed *squadristi* violence in the provinces, especially against the *Popolari* and other Catholics. Although bringing discipline to the party, his association with violence discredited the *ras* and upset those, such as Federzoni, who wanted Fascism to have a more respectable image. Farinacci's publicity-seeking role as defence counsel in the trial of Matteotti's murderers caused further embarrassment. In October, *squadristi* ran amok in Florence in front of tourists, killing innocent bystanders. This gave Mussolini ample reason to dismiss Farinacci.

Farinacci's successor, Augusto Turati, was able to make the party obedient to Mussolini, without being a driving force for Fascist revolution. He purged the membership of many 'old guard' Fascists who wanted radical changes, and allowed in new members. It became necessary to have a party card to qualify for jobs, and to gain entry to leisure facilities and social activities organised by the party. From October 1926, all posts in the PNF were appointed from above rather than elected. In 1928, the supreme body in the party, the Grand Council, legally became a part of the government. This removed any remaining impression that the Fascist Party was more powerful than the state – rather, it was now part of it.

A ONE-PARTY STATE

From January 1925 to October 1926, the main opposition parties survived in the hope that either the king would dismiss Mussolini or elections would be called. However, they had little room for manoeuvre. Newspapers that printed anything critical of the government risked confiscation. Proprietors, afraid of losing money, replaced editors who printed unflattering reports and comments. A Press Law in December 1925 made it illegal for journalists to write for newspapers unless their names were on a Fascist-controlled register. A Communist Deputy, who tried to read out evidence in Parliament of Mussolini's involvement in murder, was physically assaulted.

A fourth attempt on Mussolini's life in one year – in Bologna in October 1926 – provided a convenient excuse to withdraw all passports, to ban all opposition parties and their journals, and to set up a Special Tribunal to try terrorists and other political criminals (see margin). Mussolini himself replaced Federzoni as Interior Minister, and gave the police wide powers of arrest.

CONTROL OF THE WORKERS

One reason for the Fascists' sudden rise to power from 1920 to 1921 was their abolition of independent trades unions and co-operatives. Instead, they introduced Fascist unions, or syndicates, to represent workers' interests. By 1922, Edmondo Rossoni was leader of the Fascist unions. He wanted a system of government by mixed corporations which represented workers and employers. Such a system would force the industrialists to co-operate with the workers and lead to a more equitable society and united nation.

However, the industrialists' organisation, the *Confindustria*, strongly opposed anything that would weaken their power. In the Chigi Palace Pact of December 1923, they agreed to co-operate with Rossoni's Confederation of Fascist Syndicates, but to remain separate organisations. The industrialists did not keep to their side of the bargain. A series of strikes in 1925 led to the Vidoni Palace Pact, which made it clear that the *Confindustria* and the Rossoni Confederation were the only organisations that represented employers and workers, and that negotiated contracts and settled disputes. Workers were no longer allowed to form factory councils or to challenge the authority of the management.

In 1926, Alfredo Rocco's law on Fascist trades unions made strikes illegal. Instead, it became compulsory for workers and employers to settle their differences in labour courts. The law allowed only one organisation of workers and employers in each category of production. In July, Giuseppe Bottai became under-secretary of a new Ministry of Corporations. He produced a Charter of Labour in 1927 to guarantee justice on social issues and in labour relations. In practice, his ministry acted as arbiter in labour disputes and weakened the influence of the syndicalists. In 1928, Rossoni was sacked and his Confederation of Fascist Syndicates broken up.

The death penalty and banishment

Although the Special Tribunal had the power to impose the death penalty, there were only nine executions for political crimes between 1927 and 1940. A more usual punishment was confinement of suspects to their own homes, or banishment to remote regions or islands for up to five years.

The Charter of Labour

'The Corporative State [see pages 30–31] considers private initiative in the field of production to be the most effective and most useful instrument in the national interest ... The worker has the right to a weekly day of rest, falling on Sunday ... Breaches of discipline and acts which disturb the normal functioning of the business, committed by workers, shall be punished ... Employers must engage workmen through [the Labour Exchanges]. They have the privilege of selection within the limits of the persons enrolled in the registers of the Exchange, giving preference to members of the Fascist party ... The Fascist State proposes to accomplish: 1] The improvement of accident insurance; 2] The improvement and extension of maternity insurance; 3] Insurance against occupational illnesses; and 4] Improvement of insurance against all illness.'

From The Charter of Labour, 21 April 1927

Who stood to gain most from the Charter of Labour, and why?

Battles for the Nation

THE MEDIA AND EDUCATION

A brilliant journalist, Mussolini at first placed more faith in newspapers than in the radio and cinema. Newspapers could only print positive news – no crime, traffic accidents or scandals which might reflect badly on the government. State radio was established in 1924, but there were only 1 million wireless sets to a population of 44 million by 1939. People crowded into cafés, or into public squares to listen to radio broadcasts over public address systems. In 1926, state-sponsored newsreels became part of every cinema programme. However, film with a sound track only became technically possible a year later, and the potential of radio and film for propaganda purposes was only fully appreciated in the 1930s.

The Fascists tried, with limited success, to rival the influence of the Church over the young in schools. Infants began each school day with a prayer which opened, 'I believe in the genius of Mussolini.' Primary school textbooks taught that the Fascists had saved Italy from communist revolution, and presented Mussolini as a hero.

Indoctrination was more difficult to achieve in secondary schools. Mussolini's first Education Minister, Giovanni Gentile, disappointed Fascists as much as educationalists by championing traditional, academic education, with little room for the technical or vocational. He introduced state examinations which deliberately made it possible for only the brightest pupils to go on to secondary school and university. As a result, attendance at secondary school dropped by 100 000 within four years, and university numbers declined by 1300 by 1928.

From 1929 teachers in all state schools, and from 1931 all university professors, had to swear an oath of loyalty to the king and the Fascist regime. Of the eight Education Ministers after Gentile, only Giuseppe Bottai's School Charter of 1939 promised more status to practical subjects and vocational training. This came too late: the education system never inspired devotion to Fascism.

YOUTH ORGANISATIONS, LEISURE AND SPORT

A more systematic attempt to brainwash young people took place through youth organisations. In 1926, all Fascist youth groups became a part of the *Opera Nazionale Balilla* (ONB). Girls and boys joined from eight to 21, at which age they joined the party itself. Membership became compulsory in 1937. The emphasis was on physical fitness and parades. Summer camps were run, at which sports and pre-military training played an important role. Older age groups received political instruction. All, including the Fascist university groups (GUF), had to swear loyalty to Mussolini.

The most popular Fascist creation was the *Opera Nazionale Dopolavoro*, an after-work leisure organisation that provided clubs,

---

THE KEY ISSUES

- How did the Fascist regime try to win the hearts and minds of the Italian people?
- How successful was their strategy?

THE KEY SKILLS

Interpretation
Assessment

WHAT YOU HAVE TO DO

Judge how far Mussolini achieved his aim of making a Fascist Italy self-sufficient.

A repressive regime ...

'The regime's organisations and initiatives, which aimed at generating support and 'consent', operated in the context of a repressive atmosphere that gave a sense of compulsion to any involvement in the activities sponsored by the regime.'
Philip Morgan, Italian Fascism, 1919–1945, 1995

BENITO MUSSOLINI
ama molto i bambini.
I bimbi d'Italia amano
molto il Duce.

VIVA IL DUCE!

Saluto al Duce:

a noi!

Mussolini and child
Il Duce *as shown to children in a primary school textbook. It reads* 'Benito Mussolini loves children very much. Long live Il Duce! I salute Il Duce. To us!'

libraries, sports grounds, radios, bars, concerts, plays, circuses, virtually free summer holidays for children and organised coach trips, visits to the seaside, mountain walks and ballroom dancing. It even gave help to the poor. However, the aim of *Dopolavoro* was fun, not propaganda. The Fascist regime gained considerable popularity through sponsorship of sport, which always featured in the cinema newsreels. Motor racing, skiing, flying, cycling, athletics and football were especially encouraged. Italy won the World Cup in 1934 and 1938, as well as 12 gold medals at the Los Angeles Olympics.

ECONOMIC BATTLES

Mussolini's solutions to making Italy great were 'autarky' (economic self-sufficiency in food and raw materials), a large population and 'empire'. To achieve these, Mussolini launched a series of 'battles'.

'*The Battle for Grain*' started in 1925 following a poor harvest and a rapid rise in grain imports. The government imposed import controls on wheat and encouraged farmers to grow more cereal crops. Italy achieved self-sufficiency in grain by the late 1930s, but at a price. Protection from imports helped the less efficient farmers in the south to survive without modernising. Pasture, olive trees, citrus orchards and vineyards were ploughed up; fruit and wine exports fell significantly, and cattle and sheep numbers declined. Italy ended up by importing olive oil. Farmers in the north, on the other hand, benefited by switching from growing maize to wheat. Industrialists also prospered; for example, through tractor sales at companies such as Fiat and fertiliser production at companies such as Montecatini.

The '*Battle for the Lira*' had more to do with prestige and the need to continue importing raw materials for armaments and shipbuilding than sound economics. On 18 August 1926, Mussolini revalued the lira, so that there were 90 lira to the pound. Although this had the effect of reversing rising prices and strengthened the purchasing power of the lira abroad, it made Italian products more expensive for foreign customers. Imports of raw materials such as coal and iron for steel became cheaper, while exports such as cars fell.

Mussolini wanted a large population to provide soldiers to conquer empire and settlers to live in it. '*The Battle for Births*', launched in 1927, encouraged early marriages, forced bachelors to pay more tax, outlawed homosexuality (1931), cracked down on divorce and abortions, provided rewards for having large families and tried to exclude women from paid employment. Nevertheless, efforts to increase the birth rate failed. Moreover, as much as 28% of the industrial workforce in 1936 was female.

Meanwhile, in the '*The Battle for Land*', from 1928, controls on migration to cities from the countryside made the growing social problem of unemployment less visible and easier to police. In addition, land reclamation schemes – such as the draining of the Pontine Marshes, 56 km from Rome – created small farms and provided public works schemes for the unemployed.

Analysis of sources

Starting from the sources given above, answer the following questions:
- What does Philip Morgan mean by 'repressive atmosphere'?
- In view of Philip Morgan's comments about Mussolini's regime, how effective do you think propaganda such as the school book illustration was?

Mussolini waging 'The Battle for Grain'

'The Battle for Grain'

Why do you think Mussolini posed for the above photograph?

For class presentation

On a large piece of A3 or poster paper, write out the key headings for a class presentation which answers the question, 'Did Mussolini create more than just an authoritarian regime between 1925 and 1928?'

THE KEY ISSUES

- Why did the Pope not consistently oppose Fascism?
- Did the Fascist regime develop into something more than a repressive dictatorship during the period of the Depression?

THE KEY SKILL

Using a novel as evidence

WHAT YOU HAVE TO DO

Discover how the development of Fascism was affected by the attitude of the Vatican and the circumstances of global economic depression.

Satirising the Lateran Treaties ...

'You remember that after the peace was made between the Pope and the government the priest explained to us from the altar that a new age was beginning for the cafoni too ... And the Pope was afflicted in his heart at what he saw. So he took from the bag a whole cloud of a new kind of lice and released them over the houses of the poor saying, "Take them, my beloved children, and scratch yourselves. Thus in your idle moments you will have something to distract your thoughts from sin."'

Ignazio Silone, Fontamara, 1933

Silone was a one-time leading member of the Italian Communist Party. How would you describe and explain his attitude towards the Lateran Treaties in this quotation from his novel *Fontamara*?

The Church and the Economy

THE LATERAN PACTS

The most powerful obstacle to achieving totalitarianism was the Roman Catholic Church. From the start, Mussolini sought its blessing rather than opposition. He un-banned religious instruction in primary schools and the display of crucifixes in classrooms and law courts. Measures against abortion and contraception, and a campaign against freemasonry, won instant approval – as did the destruction of the power of the socialists. In 1923, the government rescued the Catholic Bank of Rome from financial difficulties. Furthermore, despite his reputation for atheism, Mussolini had his children baptised and, ten years after his civil wedding to Donna Rachele, had a Church wedding in 1925. Meanwhile, Pope Pius XI, accepting the Fascist ban on the *Popolari*, ordered its leader, Luigi Sturzo, into exile. Then, in 1929, Mussolini won acclaim for the Lateran Pacts, which ended the 60-year-old rift between the Church and the state, which had existed since the unification of Italy: the Vatican City became an independent, neutral state; the Church received financial compensation for land lost in 1873; Roman Catholicism became the official state religion; religious instruction was introduced in secondary schools; and Catholic Action was recognised by the state on condition that the Church directly supervised its activities. In return, the Pope formally recognised the Kingdom of Italy.

CONTINUING TENSION BETWEEN CHURCH AND STATE

Rivalry between the Catholic and Fascist Youth organisations led to the banning of the Catholic Scout movement in 1928. Suspicion that the Catholic Action organisation was a 'front' for secret political groups led by ex-*popolari* politicians led to the closing down of all offices and clubs run by Catholic Action and FUCI, the Catholic university students' organisation. The Pope vigorously protested in an open letter, in which he criticised Fascist interference in education and the rights of the family, and Fascist demands for oaths of loyalty. Later, he threatened publicly to condemn Fascism. As a result, Catholic Action and FUCI survived, but only as non-political organisations. In 1938, the Church again clashed with the government over the introduction of race laws following closer relations between Italy and Nazi Germany.

THE DEPRESSION

The world economic depression intensified the strains on the Italian people, imposed by Mussolini's drive for self-sufficiency (see page 27). By 1933, unemployment exceeded 1 million. Millions more – especially in agriculture – found only part-time work. Agricultural labourers' jobs fell by 20–40% during the worst years of the Depression. Many women had to give up their jobs to create employment for men. Compared with other countries in western Europe, however, the impact of the Great Depression on Italy was less severe.

FASCIST INTERVENTION

In 1931, the government used public money to rescue banks and businesses that had run into trouble, and in 1933 it set up the Institute of Industrial Reconstruction (IRI). This was a giant state company that took over loss-making industries. By 1939, the IRI controlled 75% of cast iron, 50% of steel production and 80% of shipping. It dominated the machine tool and electricity industries, and the telephone system. Italy became second to the Soviet Union as a state owner of industry in Europe. However, it sold off part of its stock at regular intervals and helped to concentrate ownership into fewer and larger private companies. The entire chemical industry, for example, fell into the hands of two firms, Montecatini and SINA Viscosa.

L'INQUADRAMENTO

The Fascist regime created an illusion of including, uniting and controlling all Italians. It called this process *l'inquadramento*. From 1931 to 1939, the party deliberately expanded its membership and 'capillary' organisations in an effort to incorporate the masses. Even so, by 1939 party membership included only 6% of the population. Nevertheless, the Depression gave impetus to the setting up of party welfare agencies. From 1931 to 1937, they provided a winter relief programme to coincide with the worst months of seasonal unemployment. This stimulated the development of women's *fasci*. In the course of providing welfare, the party extended its network of surveillance and control of the population through area groups and sector party social workers, who made home visits to assess and report on people's needs.

To create more employment, the government imposed a 40-hour week in industry in October 1934 and introduced family allowances to compensate industrial workers with larger families for loss of income caused by shorter hours. Meanwhile, the government maintained *Dopolavro* and public works schemes, such as the draining of the Pontine Marshes, and intensified its focus on education and youth organisations.

Mussolini with churchmen, giving the Fascist salute

Comparative effects of the Depression

Between 1929 and 1933, industrial production in Italy fell by 22.7%, whereas industrial production for western Europe as a whole between fell by 23.2%. Car production fell by 50%. Steel production fell from 2 122 000 tonnes to 1 396 000 tonnes per year.

See Chapter 4 of Philip Morgan, *Italian Fascism, 1919–1945* (Macmillan, 1995).

How the Great Depression affected Italy; what the government did to help; welfare agencies as a means of surveillance and control; *l'inquadramento*.

Freemasonry – a secret international brotherhood created for mutual assistance

Encyclical – a papal open letter to the Catholic Church worldwide, published in Latin: *Non abbiamo bisogno* was deliberately circulated in Italian because it applied specifically to Italy

Cafoni – landless peasants

Great Depression – a worldwide economic crisis sparked off by the collapse of the New York Stock Exchange on Wall Street in 1929: it caused loss of trade, bankruptcies, the closure of businesses and high unemployment

Corporativism and Propaganda

THE FASCIST 'THIRD WAY'

Mussolini created a Ministry of Corporations in July 1926, headed by himself until 1929, when the job went to his under-secretary, Bottai (see page 25 for his 1927 Charter of Labour). Bottai established a National Council of Corporations in March 1930, which comprised seven large corporations representing the main branches of the economy. In 1932, Mussolini reassumed personal control, and in 1934 the NCC grew to 22. Each corporation consisted of councils of workers' and employers' representatives, who met in the presence of party or ministry officials, thus representing the national interest. In 1939, a Chamber of Corporations and *Fasci* replaced Parliament: Italy was, in name at least, a Corporative State.

In theory, corporativism abolished class conflict and labour disputes by bringing employers and workers together, the state or party acting as referees. The corporations fixed the price of goods and services in their own areas, ensuring disciplined working conditions in the interests of economic efficiency. Significantly, Mussolini's resumption of control of the Ministry of Corporations coincided with a general ministerial shake-up, in which he also took back foreign affairs and strengthened his dictatorship.

To celebrate ten years in power, the Fascists sponsored an international conference at Volta to promote Fascism. This was followed in 1934 by the launch of a Fascist 'International' of European movements. The Fascist Corporative State was projected as a 'third way', as distinct from communism and liberal capitalism. By this time, Mussolini had fully realised the power of cinema and radio to promote his position as *Duce* of Fascism and celebrate his achievements in Italy.

THE REALITY OF THE CORPORATIVE STATE

In reality, the employers were the only side genuinely represented in the corporations. Workers' representatives were generally not close to the workers, but were picked by the party or Ministry of Corporations. Tending to be middle-class men with careers as Fascist Party or syndicalist officials, they got on well with employers. The corporations' decisions had to be approved from above, and there was considerable red tape and corruption. Corporation officials earned higher salaries than civil servants but often duplicated their work.

Nearly all policy decisions in response to the Depression bypassed the corporations. These included, where there was a majority of firms in favour, the compulsory forming of a business consortium intended to restrict competition and prevent prices from falling. At the same time, the government cut wages. The IRI (see page 29) and the *Confindustria* continued to exist independently of the corporative system.

THE KEY ISSUES

- Who benefited most from the Corporative State, and why?
- What do propaganda images of Mussolini tell us about the nature of his dictatorship?

THE KEY SKILLS

Evaluation of evidence and interpretation
Analysis of pictorial images

WHAT YOU HAVE TO DO

Understand how far the creation of the Corporative State and the cult of *Il Duce* were central to Fascism and beneficial to the Italian people.

A view of 'corporativism' ...

'Perhaps one idea which the Duce himself never took very seriously was the concept of corporativism, but as the supreme 'Editor-in Chief' he realised its propaganda value at home and abroad, and as an astute politician he saw the practical advantages which it offered.'

John Whittam,
Fascist Italy, 1995

For discussion and debate

'The Corporative State was a genuine attempt to create an alternative to both the communist and capitalist methods of managing the economy.' Discuss.

Even the Fascist trades unions (syndicates) survived, although their role was more one of collaboration. For example, in 1934 the syndicates persuaded the government to introduce the 40-hour week – a measure which reduced by 10% the monthly wages of those already in work. Nevertheless, the creation of the Corporative State was a highly successful propaganda exercise, attracting the attention of political scientists, economists and sociologists the world over.

THE CULT OF *IL DUCE*

From the outset, the Press Office carefully controlled the public image of Mussolini. Newspapers projected him as a dynamic, energetic and ageless leader. Photographs emphasised his virility and sporting prowess, as well as his cultured side (see margin). He was one of the first politicians to be heard speaking on film, and chose to show off his language skills by using English. In 1933 his son-in-law, Galeazzo Ciano, took over the Press Office and turned it, in 1935, into the Ministry for Press and Propaganda. In 1937, it became the Ministry of Popular Culture, or *Minculpop*.

Achille Starace, Party Secretary from 1930, promoted the hero worship of Mussolini and the wearing of uniforms. He would run to Mussolini's desk at the start of a meeting and stand to attention when speaking to him on the telephone. Mussolini's picture was everywhere – in public buildings, shops, offices and on the streets. Catchphrases such as 'Believe, obey, fight!' ('*Credere, obbedire, combattere!*') and 'Mussolini is always right!' were stencilled on walls across Italy.

Film newsreel relayed Mussolini's public appearances before apparently adoring crowds. Carefully chosen camera angles conveyed a sense of his authority, disguising the fact that he was not very tall. At press conferences he would arrive with an escort of Blackshirts, and a team nicknamed 'the applause squad' accompanied him on official visits.

ROMANITA

Mussolini encouraged the link in people's minds between Fascist Italy and Ancient Rome. Fascist academics, writers and artists promoted the age of Fascism as the revival of Italy as the centre of civilisation. They presented Mussolini as a reincarnation of one of the Caesars, and the Fascist Party attempted to popularise the Roman salute as being more hygienic than a handshake or kiss. However, the adoption in 1938 by the Italian army of *passo romano*, the 'goose-step', was seen as evidence of the growing influence of Nazi Germany (see page 38). Mussolini was known as *Il Duce* (Latin for 'leader') and the *fasces*, the bundle of rods and an axe that symbolised authority in Ancient Rome, became the Fascist emblem. Few outspoken critics of Fascism were tolerated. The notable exception was the philosopher, Croce. As his influence was not great, such toleration was evidence of intellectual freedom in Fascist Italy.

Mussolini with his pet lioness, 'Italia'

Mussolini on a motorcycle

Mussolini playing the violin

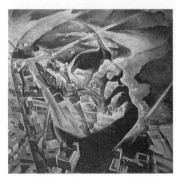
Mussolini glorified – a modernist painting

Analysing propaganda

Describe the propaganda purposes of the images of Mussolini shown in the above pictures, and list examples of possible propaganda images not shown.

Manoeuvring for Position: 1922–1931

Foreign Secretaries

1922–1929	Benito Mussolini
1929–1932	Dino Grandi
1932–1936	Benito Mussolini
1936–1943	Galeazzo Ciano

In reality, Mussolini controlled policy-making throughout.

Chapter 5 of Alan Cassels, *Fascist Italy* (Routledge and Kegan Paul, 1969), titled 'Fascist Diplomacy', provides a very accessible overview. Denis Mack Smith, *Mussolini's Roman Empire* (1976), presents Mussolini as a posturing, unsystematic, careless opportunist, who falls victim to his own brilliant propaganda. Esmonde M. Robertson, *Mussolini as Empire-builder: Europe and Africa 1932–36* (Macmillan, 1977), puts forward the view that Mussolini tried to pursue a systematic policy. The introduction includes a useful review of interpretations. There is an excellent chronological table at the back.

BOXED IN

Between 1922 and 1931, Mussolini had limited room for manoeuvre. His aim was to make Italy the key to the balance of power in Europe by dominating the Mediterranean. However, the creation of Yugoslavia in the 1919 peace settlement and the control of strategic positions in the Mediterranean by Britain and France (see map) boxed Italy in. A further obstacle was the League of Nations, created to deter aggression by the collective action of its members.

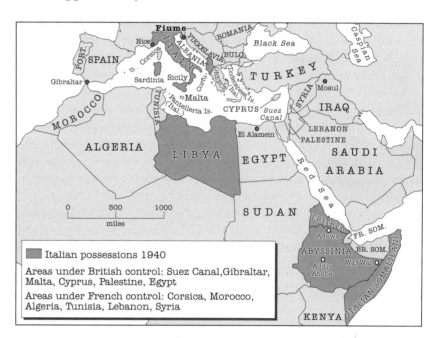

Italy, Europe and North Africa, 1919–1940

INTRIGUE AND OPPORTUNISM

1922   Mussolini made unofficial contacts with German nationalists opposed to the Weimar Republic. A destabilised Germany would give Italy greater security and room for manoeuvre in eastern Europe.

1923   The Italian navy bombarded and landed marines on the island of Corfu. This followed Greece's refusal to apologise and pay L50 million in compensation for the murder on Greek soil of four Italians who were working for the League of Nations along the Greek–Albanian border. Pressure from Britain forced Italy to withdraw, but Greece paid the L50 million.

In the same year, Mussolini began to cultivate good relations with Spain's new leader, General Miguel Primo de Rivera, in the hope of making him an ally against Britain and France. Meanwhile, he opened diplomatic and trading links with Communist Russia and supported Abyssinia's application to join the League of Nations.

DIPLOMAT OR TROUBLEMAKER?

1924 Mussolini achieved through diplomacy what D'Annunzio had failed to achieve by force – Italian occupation of Fiume, with the agreement of Yugoslavia. Italy officially recognised the USSR. Mussolini secretly supplied financial aid to the Nazis in Germany.

1925 Mussolini took part in the Locarno agreement, whereby Germany agreed to respect its borders with Belgium and France. Although his role was presented to the Italian public as a personal triumph, Mussolini was secretly unhappy at the lack of a similar guarantee of the Austrian and Italian frontier. He began talks with Britain over the future of Abyssinia. Although not official policy, Mussolini spoke openly of Fascism spreading to other countries.

1926 Italy made Albania an Italian Protectorate. Britain gave a portion of the Juba Valley in Kenya to Italian Somalia and made Egypt give up the Oasis of Jarabub to Libya. Mussolini allowed rebels against the government of Yugoslavia to set a terrorist training school in Parma.

1927 Mussolini signed a Pact of Friendship with Hungary, in sympathy with Hungarian hopes to revise the peace treaties – which he broke by secretly sending arms to Hungary and to paramilitary organisations in Germany, Bulgaria and Austria. Yugoslavia sought protection in a system of alliances with France, Czechoslovakia and Romania, known as the 'Little Entente'.

1928 Mussolini signed a treaty of friendship with Abyssinia, despite hostile intentions, and supported an international pact, sponsored by the USA and France, to outlaw war.

1929 Renewing calls to revise the 1919 peace treaties, Mussolini intrigued with Hungary to overthrow King Alexander of Yugoslavia. At a conference in London, on international disarmament, Italy refused to agree to the Italian navy being restricted to anything less than those of Britain or France. However, tensions did not prevent discussion with France over Abyssinia. Meanwhile, Italian fascists in Malta, where Britain had a naval base, stirred up trouble against the British presence.

1931 Britain and France failed to back military action by the League of Nations in response to Japan's invasion of Manchuria. The conclusions to be drawn were not lost on Mussolini.

Mussolini's image abroad

No mention was made in the Italian press of the fact that hundreds of foreign journalists boycotted Mussolini's appearance at the signing of the 1925 Locarno Treaties, in protest against Fascist brutality in Italy.

Austen Chamberlain, the British Foreign Secretary, admired Mussolini's anti-Bolshevism and referred to him in 1924 as 'a wonderful man working for the greatness of his country'. His wife, Lady Chamberlain, took to wearing the Fascist badge.

Problems and solutions

How does the map opposite show the obstacles to Italy achieving greater power in eastern Europe, the Mediterranean and North Africa? How useful was foreign policy as a diversion from political crisis or as a means of achieving autarky?

What Mussolini wanted to achieve; limited room for manoeuvre; Corfu 1923; Fiume 1924; Locarno 1925; intrigues to undermine the peace settlements; the Little Entente; the treaty of friendship with Abyssinia; Japan's invasion of Manchuria.

'The Doormat', by David Low

The League of Nations

How does the above cartoon illustrate that Japan's occupation of Manchuria exposed the weakness of the League of Nations? What does this cartoon tell us about how public opinion was formed about the League of Nations?

Mussolini's Four-power Pact; German rearmament; the 1934 murder of Dollfuss.

Invasion plans

Why might Germany's withdrawal from the League of Nations and rearmament have brought forward Mussolini's plans to invade Abyssinia?

Empire-builder: 1932–1935

A FOUR-POWER PACT PROPOSED

In January 1933, as Hitler came to power in Germany, reports appeared in an Austrian socialist newspaper about Italy supplying arms to the right-wing Austrian *Heimwehr* and the *Ustaši*, a Croat terrorist organisation in Hungary.

Czechoslovakia, Romania and Yugoslavia demanded action by the League of Nations. Britain and France got Italy off the hook by making Austria responsible for destroying or returning the weapons. Because of this, the Little Entente strengthened its resolve to stand up to Mussolini, giving him grounds to fear a preventative war against him. Mussolini countered in 1934 by increasing trade links and seeking common ground on foreign policy with Austria and Hungary. Meanwhile, he attempted to displace the League of Nations by inviting Germany, Britain and France to join Italy in a Four-power Pact. Significantly, only Germany showed an interest, and soon German pilots were being trained in Italy.

HITLER

Germany's withdrawal from the League of Nations and Hitler's well known intentions to expand into eastern Europe made Mussolini apprehensive.

Eastern European powers including the USSR had reason to feel insecure too. In September 1933, the USSR persuaded Mussolini to agree to a non-aggression pact. Then, in July 1934, Mussolini was outraged by the murder of the Austrian Chancellor, Engelbert Dollfuss, by Austrian Nazis. Dollfuss' wife and children happened to be staying with Mussolini's family at the time. He reacted swiftly and decisively by sending Italian troops to the Austrian border to deter any possibility of a German-sponsored takeover of Austria. Mussolini's apparent willingness to restrain Hitler impressed Britain and France, despite the assassination in October 1934 in Marseilles of the French Foreign Minister and King Alexander of Yugoslavia by Croat terrorists, supplied with arms and weapons by the Italian government. Hitler's denunciation of the disarmament clauses of the Versailles peace settlement and the introduction of conscription in March 1935 gave Italy an opportunity – at a conference at Stresa in the following April – to demonstrate a united front with France and Britain against Germany's defiant behaviour.

A FREE HAND IN ABYSSINIA

Mussolini judged correctly that his attendance at the Stresa conference might favourably influence the attitude of Britain and France to his plans to conquer Abyssinia, which he had drawn up as early as 1932. Indeed, in January France had given up part of French Somaliland and sold its share in the Abyssinian railway to Italy, and in June Mussolini obtained a copy of a report prepared for the British government by Sir John Maffey, which concluded that Britain did not have vital interests in Abyssinia that would make it worth resisting an Italian conquest. It seemed that all that was required was a convenient incident to provide an excuse to put his plans for invasion into action. This was successfully engineered in December 1934, when some Italians were killed by Abyssinians who were resisting Italy's right to use, as a military base, the oasis of Wal Wal, which was 130 km inside the border between Abyssinia and Italian Somaliland. Abyssinia's appeal to the League of Nations secured an agreement to an investigation in May 1935, but did not deter the Italian invasion, which began on 3 October.

CONQUEST AND CONSEQUENCES

The Abyssinians stood little chance against a force of half a million Italian servicemen, equipped with modern weapons, aircraft and poisonous gas. In December 1935, the press got hold of a proposed plan by the British and French Foreign Secretaries, Sir Samuel Hoare and Pierre Laval, to offer two-thirds of Abyssinia to Italy. This outraged British public opinion and led to Hoare's dismissal. Britain and France were embarrassed into supporting League of Nations sanctions. Nevertheless, the new British Foreign Secretary, Anthony Eden, pressed in vain for oil to be added to the list of economic sanctions, which also excluded coal, iron and steel and kept the Suez Canal open to Italian shipping. The ineffective nature of the sanctions served only to help whip up a patriotic reaction in Italy and did not expose the failings of the drive towards autarky. The invasion was over in nine months. Mussolini reached the height of his popularity in Italy. The Catholic Church regarded the conquest as a civilising mission. Women, including the Queen of Italy, donated their gold wedding rings as contributions to the cost.

However, the conquest of Abyssinia was turning point in Italy's relations with Germany. In January 1936, Mussolini informed Hitler that he no longer objected to Austria becoming a German satellite. He hinted that he would not oppose German troops entering the Rhineland, and on 6 March he decided to withdraw Italy from the League of Nations and adopt a pro-German policy.

WHEN KNIGHTS ARE BOLD.
"IT'S YOUR OWN FAULT. A CIVILISED MAN MUST PROTECT HIMSELF—AND WHAT'S MORE, IT'S BEGINNING TO RAIN."

'When knights are bold'
From Punch, 15 January 1935

The Hoare–Laval Pact

How does the appearance of the above cartoon in a popular British magazine help explain public outrage at the Hoare–Laval Pact?

French concessions to Italy in East Africa; the Maffey Report; Italy's military advantages over Abyssinia; the Hoare–Laval Pact; Mussolini withdraws objections to Austria becoming a German satellite.

International relations

In what sense was Italy's conquest of Abyssinia a turning point in international relations?

THE KEY ISSUES

- Why did Mussolini change policy over Austria's independence?
- What did Mussolini aim to achieve by the Rome–Berlin Axis?
- To what extent did Mussolini begin to lose popularity inside Italy as a result of involvement in the Spanish Civil War?

THE KEY SKILLS

Interpretation
Argument
Testing a hypothesis

WHAT YOU HAVE TO DO

Critically examine Mussolini's reasons for developing closer relations with Germany. Discover why Mussolini involved Italy in the Spanish Civil War, and examine the economic, political and diplomatic consequences.

An example of historians in debate

The Italian historian, Renzo De Felice, interpreted the Rome–Berlin Axis as a 'blackmailer's card' to extract concessions from France and Britain. Philip Morgan, on the other hand, argues that 'the Axis indicated that Mussolini had made a choice' to align Italy with Germany. Whose interpretation do you agree with?

See Robert Mallett, *The Italian Navy and Fascist Expansionism 1935–40* (Frank Cass, 1998), Philip Morgan, *Italian Fascism, 1919–45* (Macmillan, 1995) and Renzo De Felice, *Mussolini il Duce, 2: Lo stato totalitario 1936–1940* (1981).

Anschluss *and the Spanish Civil War*

POLICY CHANGE OVER AUSTRIA

At their first meeting, in Venice in June 1934, Mussolini had not been impressed by Hitler. However, Hitler made clear his ambition to start a European war by attacking France before the French had time to mobilise. Significantly, Hitler left Venice with the impression that Mussolini did not object to a pro-Nazi government in Austria. Driven by ambition for empire, Mussolini came to accept that an *Anschluss* was a price worth paying to avoid diplomatic isolation for invading Abyssinia. What he required from Hitler was time to prepare the Italian people, because the reaction to an *Anschluss* might threaten his very survival.

Therefore, Mussolini expressed outrage over the murder of Dollfuss by Austrian Nazis in July 1934, and continued to support Austria's independence. But, by 6 January 1936, he was ready to do a U-turn, because of the League-imposed sanctions on Italy. Mussolini let Hitler know that Italy no longer objected to Austria becoming a satellite of Germany.

FEARS OF A FASCIST ALLIANCE

The Germans refused to apply sanctions – and became a major supplier of materials and energy crucial to Italy's survival. In March Hitler took advantage of the situation to reoccupy the remainder of the Rhineland. This broke the Treaty of Versailles and the Locarno agreements. Mussolini reciprocated by declaring that he would not support possible League action against Germany.

The sanctions that the League of Nations imposed on Italy reflected Britain and France's fears of an alliance between Italy and Germany. For this reason, two vital elements were excluded from the sanctions: oil and access through the Suez Canal. Thus Italy completed its conquest of Abyssinia without serious hindrance. And, when sanctions were lifted in July 1936, Mussolini claimed victory over the 50 nations that had supported them.

THE ROME–BERLIN AXIS

The invasion of Abyssinia was a watershed in Italian foreign policy. Germany and Italy were soon co-operating on a number of issues: Germany joined Italy in stirring up trouble among the Arabs in British-ruled Palestine; the Italian and German secret police agreed to co-operate, although this did yet not include joint surveillance of Jews; a common front was formed against communism; and they agreed parallel spheres of influence in Europe, Italy in the Mediterranean and the Balkans, and Germany in northern and eastern-central Europe.

They also sent military aid to a rebellion in Spain against the Republican government, which led to the outbreak of the Spanish Civil

War in July 1936. On 1 November, Mussolini described Italy's relations with Germany as an 'axis around which all the European states animated by the will to collaboration and peace can also collaborate'.

THE SPANISH CIVIL WAR

In July 1936 in Spain, a conservative alliance of army officers, landowners, industrialists, monarchists, clergy and the *Falange* (the Spanish Fascist party) rebelled against the newly elected Popular Front government, a Republican alliance of socialists, trades unions, liberals and left-wing radicals. Mussolini was afraid that the new Popular Front government in France, led by Léon Blum, would send an army across the Pyrenees to crush the revolt, and that Spain would become a French satellite.

The possibility of installing a pro-Fascist government in Spain excited him. Not only might it lead to the use of the Balearic Islands as Italian naval bases, but also to the removal of the British naval base at Gibraltar. Russian aid to the Republicans (among whom communists were prominent) and German military aid to Franco, the leader of the Nationalist rebels, became additional reasons for Italian involvement.

Italy's military commitment was extravagant compared with that of the Russians and Germans. Mussolini staked his prestige at home and abroad on victory for the rebels. Their leader, General Francisco Franco, was not a Fascist, but he presented his rebellion as a religious crusade against communism and won the blessing of the Pope. This made it easier for Mussolini to commit Italians to fight in another war so soon after the conquest of Abyssinia.

REACTION AT HOME AND ABROAD

Unlike the Abyssinian war, involvement in Spain did not enhance Mussolini's domestic popularity. The Spanish campaign dragged on, at immense cost to the Italian people. Most of this was sent on credit and was not paid for by the Nationalists. In contrast, the Republicans paid for Russian supplies out of their dwindling gold reserves. Italian anti-Fascists in exile fought on the Republicans' side and played a part in defeating Italian troops who were fighting for Franco at the Battle of Guadalajara in March 1937. On reaching Italy, this embarrassing news greatly encouraged opponents of the Fascist regime, such as Carlo Rosselli. The slogan 'Today in Spain, tomorrow in Italy' began to appear on walls. Within three months, Mussolini's secret agents had assassinated Rosselli and his brother in France.

Britain and France did not come to the rescue of the Republicans in Spain. Their policy of non-intervention was more helpful to the rebels. Fear of the war in Spain escalating into a major European war explains their restraint when Italian submarines sank British, French, Greek and Danish cargo ships; and when Italian aircraft bombed British and French shipping in Spanish ports. Mussolini drew the conclusion that the European democracies were unwilling to fight, even when attacked. Nevertheless, these acts of aggression turned influential opinion in Britain and France against Italy.

Italian assistance in Spain

During the Spanish Civil War, Mussolini sent vast quantities of raw materials to Spain: 1400 pilots, 400 fighter planes, 200 bombers and over 70 000 ground troops fought on the rebels' side. Altogether, Italian assistance cost L7500 million.

Testing a hypothesis

This activity involves the testing of a hypothesis. You must examine the available evidence and then construct an argument that reaches a conclusion on the issue in question.

Hypothesis: 'Italy's involvement in the Spanish Civil War was a turning point in Mussolini's popularity.'

Questions to ask yourself when testing the hypothesis:
- Do we really know how popular Mussolini was before 1936?
- What effect upon Mussolini's prestige did involvement in the Spanish Civil War have, compared with the conquest of Abyssinia?

Task: Construct an argument for or against the hypothesis.

Satellite – a country controlled by another

Anschluss – the German word for 'union' (in this case, between Germany and Austria)

THE KEY ISSUE

- What did Mussolini's acceptance of the *Anschluss* indicate about the true nature of relations between Italy and Germany?

THE KEY SKILLS

Analysis and interpretation

WHAT YOU HAVE TO DO

Make a judgement about whether Germany had, by this stage, become the dominant partner in relations with Italy.

GOOD HUNTING

Mussolini. "All right, Adolf—I never heard a shot"

'Good Hunting'
A comment on the Anschluss from a British point of view (Punch, 1938)

Mussolini versus Hitler

What does the above cartoon suggest about how the British interpreted Mussolini's role in Germany's invasion of Austria? Does it show Mussolini and Hitler as equals, or is one the more dominant?

The Impact of the Axis on Italy

SIGNS OF GERMAN INFLUENCE

Had Mussolini finally made a choice? Was a formal alliance between Italy and Germany inevitable? During a four-day visit by the *Duce* to Germany in September 1937, Hitler went out of his way to impress Mussolini with evidence of Germany's industrial and military might. Mussolini, flattered by his reception, made it clear again that he would accept an *Anschluss* with Austria. He also said that he was putting into practice a tough policy of anti-Semitism.

In December 1937, Italy joined the Anti-Comintern Pact, earlier signed in November 1936 by Germany and Japan to combat the strategies of the Communist International. At this stage Mussolini resisted a formal alliance with Germany. On the one hand, he wished to preserve the impression of Italy's independence; on the other, he was sensitive to Italian fears of Germany becoming the dominant partner in the growing friendship. Such fears were aroused by scenes such as Mussolini personally demonstrating the *passo romano* (the 'goose-step') to Italian soldiers.

ANSCHLUSS 1938

Italy's relationship with Germany was put to the test in March 1938 when, with only a few hours' notice, Germany invaded and took over Austria. The suddenness of Hitler's action took Mussolini by surprise: Hitler had promised him sufficient warning in order to prepare the Italian public. Nevertheless, Mussolini did nothing. Hitler sent him a telegram: '*Mussolini – ich werde Ihnen dieses nie vergessen*'. ('Mussolini – I shall never forget you for this.') This was one of the few promises that Hitler kept.

DOMESTIC AWARENESS OF MUSSOLINI'S VULNERABILITY

In April 1938, Mussolini signed a pact of friendship with Britain. Britain recognised the Italian Empire in exchange for a commitment to withdraw from Spain. It was intended, and interpreted, as a signal that Mussolini did not want to burn all his boats with 'the other side'. When Hitler came to Italy in May to repay Mussolini's 1937 visit, he was disappointed not to secure a formal alliance.

Mussolini made every effort to organise a display to match what he had seen in Germany. The Italians, and in particular the army leaders, were painfully aware that it was all an illusion. Houses along the route on which Hitler was taken were either specially repainted or pulled down and replaced by façades. Even some of the trees were false. Despite the boasting in the Italian newspapers of new types of weapons, some of the armoured cars carried wooden guns. Hitler returned home with only general assurances of Italian support, particularly with regard to his increasingly aggressive policy towards Czechoslovakia.

THE MUNICH CRISIS 1938

The crisis provoked by Hitler's threat to invade Czechoslovakia in September 1938 allowed Mussolini to pose as peace-maker. At a special conference in Munich, he assisted in a deal between Germany and the democracies of the West, who put pressure on Czechoslovakia to cede the Sudetenland to Germany. Meanwhile, anticipating that negotiations would fail and planning to take advantage of a German attack on Czechoslovakia, Mussolini ordered the Italian navy to prepare for war against Britain in the Mediterranean.

ANTI-SEMITISM

Until the Rome–Berlin Axis, racism was not a strong feature of Italian Fascism. Mussolini had a Jewish mistress, Margherita Sarfatti, and appointed a Jewish Minister of Finance, Guido Jung, between 1932 and 1935. Senior Fascists including Balbo (who had close links with the Jewish community in Ferrara), De Bono, Federzoni, Gentile and Marinetti disapproved of the racial laws that Mussolini suddenly introduced between September and November 1938. Pope Pius XI condemned them, accusing Mussolini of breaking the Concordat of 1929 and of aping the Germans.

Enforcement of the laws was, at first, half-hearted. Most Italians were sympathetic to the Jews and were prepared to help them. Even Mussolini helped his former mistress to escape to Argentina in 1939. Extreme persecution of Italian Jews did not begin until 1943. But Mussolini's introduction of anti-Semitic laws was not just the result of German influence. There was a racist element in the *Romanità* movement (see page 33), which emphasised Italy's Roman heritage. Mussolini's 'Battle for Births' (to provide future soldiers and settlers for the re-creation of the Roman Empire) and his belief in war as a means of strengthening the Italian race were both reinforced by victories against the black tribes of Abyssinia. Moreover, Mussolini felt the need to impress the countries of eastern Europe with anti-Semitic credentials in order to counter the attractions for them of Nazi Germany.

THE PACT OF STEEL 1939

The outcome of the Munich Conference finally convinced Mussolini of the weakness of Britain and France. In March 1939, Germany took over the remainder of Czechoslovakia. Not to be outdone, Italy formally annexed Albania in April, despite the fact that it was already under Italian control. Britain and France responded to both acts of aggression by guaranteeing to support Poland, Greece and Romania. In May, Mussolini suddenly agreed to a formal alliance with Germany –the Pact of Steel–which committed both countries to assist each other in the event of war. Although he relished the prospect of war, which he now saw as inevitable, Mussolini believed that Hitler understood that Italy would not be ready until 1943.

Anti-Semitic laws in Italy

Jews were expelled from the Fascist Party, the civil service, the armed forces, the professions and cultural establishments. Jewish children were excluded from non-Jewish schools and banned from mixing with 'Aryans'. Mixed marriages became illegal, and foreign-born Jews who had become Italian citizens since 1919 lost their right to live in Italy.

Mussolini's reaction to Pope Pius XI's criticism of his race laws

'Those who try to make out that we have simply imitated, or worse, that we have been obedient to suggestions, are poor fools whom we do not know whether to pity or despise. The racial problem has not broken out suddenly. It is related to our conquest of our empire; for history teaches us that empires are won by arms but held by prestige. And prestige demands a clear-cut consciousness which is based not only on difference but on the most definite superiority. The Jewish problem is thus merely one aspect of this phenomenon ...'

Benito Mussolini, speaking on 18 September 1938

Review this page by answering the following questions:
- What did Mussolini possibly hope to gain from the Czech crisis of 1938?
- Why did Mussolini introduce racial laws?

Delayed Entry into the War

THE KEY ISSUES

- How did Mussolini's preparation of the Italian people for war affect relations with the Church and the king?
- Why was Italy unprepared for war in 1939?

THE KEY SKILL

Analysis of causation

WHAT YOU HAVE TO DO

Throughout this chapter, identify the reasons for Mussolini's downfall. Analyse the reasons for Italy's economic and military weakness.

Relations with the Pope and the king

Measures to increase Fascist control and make a totalitarian dictatorship upset both the Pope and the king. Neither was happy about what they saw as the growing influence of Germany, resulting from the Axis. The Pope's condemnation of the race laws reflected only a part of the growing tension between Church and state. The Fascists saw Catholic Action as a rival competing for influence. Fascist Party and police harassment of those involved in Catholic Action antagonised the Pope.

At the same time, Mussolini gave the king good cause to suspect his intention eventually to abolish the monarchy. In January 1939, he replaced the Chamber of Elected Deputies with a government-appointed Chamber of Fasces and Corporations. This became the new law-making body and appeared to leave the king out of the process altogether. The king remained commander-in-chief of the armed forces, but only just. On the eve of Italian intervention in the war, he gave in to pressure to allow Mussolini command of operational, but not all, armed forces.

PREPARATION OF ITALY FOR WAR

To Mussolini's disappointment, it was difficult to convert all Italians to the Fascist belief that war was natural. After the invasion of Abyssinia, efforts to make Italians Fascist intensified. The Ministry of Press and Propaganda became the Ministry of Popular Culture in May 1937, in an effort to achieve full control of all cultural activity. In the same year, the Fascist Party took control of the youth organisation, *Opera Nazionale Balilla*, and merged it with the Young Fascists to form *Gioventù Italiana del Littorio* (GIL). In this way, the party aimed to organise and indoctrinate both sexes between the ages of six and 21.

GIL instructors ran all sports activities and physical education in state elementary and secondary schools, and also organised pre-military training for 8- to 18-year-olds. In 1940, a government and party working group recommended that GIL activities should take up every afternoon of the school day. However, wartime commitments made this impractical to implement. Nevertheless, ideas of racial superiority and attacks on beliefs such as democracy and pacifism became a part of the school curriculum. The raised arm of the Fascist salute replaced the 'unhygienic' handshake as a form of greeting. Fascists insisted on using the direct word for 'you' in Italian (*'voi'*) instead of the polite and formal *'lei'*. State officials began to wear uniform.

Mussolini told his son-in-law, Galeazzo Ciano, in July 1938:

'Henceforth, the revolution must impinge upon the habits of the Italians. They must learn to be less sympathetic in order to become hard, relentless and hateful – in other words, masters.'

It greatly annoyed Mussolini when Italians expressed enthusiasm for his peace-keeping role at Munich in September 1938, during the Czech crisis.

MUSSOLINI DELAYED

The so-called Pact of Steel, signed in May 1939, committed both countries to consult each other on all matters and agree joint military action where desired. It was soon clear, however, that the Germans had no intention of informing Italy in advance of their every move. In March 1939, Germany occupied the Czech provinces of Bohemia and Moravia. Mussolini complained privately, 'Every time Hitler occupies a country he sends me a message.'

Nevertheless, he continued to defend vigorously the need to remain loyal to Germany despite the king's disapproval and outspoken criticism from *ras* such as Balbo, who remarked 'You are licking Germany's boots'. Mussolini's loyalty to the Axis remained unshaken despite the surprise news in August of a non-aggression pact between Germany and their common enemy, Russia. When it became clear that Hitler intended to attack Poland and risk war with Britain and France, the king was horrified:

'In his judgement we are absolutely in no condition to wage war. The Army is in a "pitiful" state. The military review and the manoeuvres have fully revealed the unhappy state of the unpreparedness of all our major formations.'

Foreign Secretary Ciano, from a diary entry for 24 August 1939

Mussolini reluctantly bowed to pressure to delay Italy's entry into the war in September 1939, but agreed to send agricultural and industrial workers to Germany.

ITALY'S UNREADINESS FOR WAR

From 1935 to 1939, government spending rocketed from about L30 billion to L60 billion. This increased the government's debt from about L2 billion to L28 billion. By 1939, between a quarter and a third of all spending was on the armed forces and industries linked to preparation for war. Mussolini's aim was autarky (economic self-sufficiency). However, dependence on imports of coal, oil and raw materials made this unattainable. Autarky could only be achieved by war and conquest – the appropriation of *spazio vitale* (living space).

Mussolini boasted that Italy's air force was so large that it could blot out the sun, that Italy could summon up 'eight million bayonets', and that the Italian navy could control the Mediterranean. He should have known better. After all, from 1933, Mussolini was the minister of all three armed forces. However, in order to keep the support of the military leaders, he left them alone to run their own affairs. Early in 1925, he had bowed to pressure from the more conservative generals to abandon radical proposals for restructuring and modernisation. Consequently, the air force had no long-range bombers, and the navy lacked a fleet air arm and aircraft carriers. Actions in Abyssinia, Spain and then in Albania used up much of the huge investment in military resources between 1935 and 1939. Mussolini took the title, 'First Marshal of the Empire' in 1938, but no serious effort was made to coordinate the three services.

'The Three Sowings' by Carpanetti

Production of armaments

How Italy compared with other countries (in billions of US dollars):

	1940	1941	1943
Great Britain	3.5	6.5	11.1
Germany	6.0	6.0	13.8
Japan	1.0	2.0	4.5
Italy	0.75	1.0	–

From Paul Kennedy, The Rise and Fall of the Great Powers (Fontana, 1988)

The Pact of Steel ?

- Why, despite Italy's unreadiness for war, did Mussolini commit Italy to the Pact of Steel in May 1939?
- Was Mussolini the victim of his own propaganda, or was he deceived by the leaders of the armed forces?
- Was Mussolini ultimately responsible for Italy's unreadiness for war in September 1939?

'The Three Sowings' ?

- How does the painting opposite reflect the Fascist belief that war was completely natural?
- What evidence is there that Italians failed to be convinced of this?

THE KEY ISSUES

- What errors of judgement by Mussolini contributed to Italy's military disasters?
- Was the German invasion of Russia in 1941 the key to Mussolini's downfall or was Mussolini more to blame himself?

THE KEY SKILLS

Analysis and selection
Interpretation and evaluation

WHAT YOU HAVE TO DO

Judge how far Mussolini's conduct of the Second World War and Italy's alliance with Germany contributed to Italy's defeat.

Errors of judgement

Taking into consideration Italy's unreadiness for war, find five examples of errors of judgement by Mussolini which contributed to military setbacks for Italy and drained the resources of Germany.

Hitler's views on Mussolini

'If he had wanted to pick a fight, why did he not attack Malta or Crete? It would at least make some sense in the context of war with Britain in the Mediterranean.'

Adolf Hitler, quoted in R. Collier, The Years of Attrition, 1940–41 (Allison & Busby, 1995)

Starting with the above quotation, answer the following two questions:

- How do you explain Hitler's bewilderment?
- How do you explain Mussolini's different course of action?

Military Disaster

MUSSOLINI'S EARLY STRATEGY

For a while, after the collapse of Poland, there was a tense pause before the real war began. This period, known as the Phoney War, seemed to justify the postponement of Italy's entry. Then, in the spring of 1940, Hitler won a series of stunning victories as German forces swept through Holland, Belgium and France. Already embarrassed by delay and anxious not to lose out while pickings remained, Mussolini declared war on 10 June 1940.

Mussolini intended to fight a 'parallel war' to assert Italy's independent status and establish the Mediterranean as its sphere of influence. He wanted the war to have a revolutionary effect inside Italy, which would place him in an unchallengeable position to sweep aside those institutions which limited his power – the Church and the monarchy in particular. To the bewilderment of Hitler, he chose not to strike at Malta and destroy British naval power in the Mediterranean as his first strategic objective. Instead, he sent troops over the Alps into France, in a bid to press Italian claims before France signed an armistice, following its surrender to Germany. Italy gained little apart from unnecessary Italian casualties – mostly from frostbite. Next, Italy conquered British Somaliland (in August) and advanced on Egypt and the Suez Canal (in September), before attempting a disastrous invasion of Greece in late October.

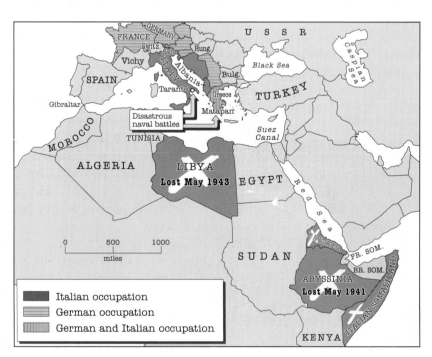

Mussolini's war, 1940–1943

THE INVASION OF GREECE

The attack on Greece was prompted by Germany's occupation of Romania, which had been planned by Hitler in order to take exclusive control of its oil fields. Mussolini was afraid that this was part of a plan to achieve German dominance in the Balkans. However, Mussolini also wanted to repay Hitler for his lack of consultation. He had complained:

> 'Hitler always presents me with a *fait accompli*. He will find out from the newspapers that I have occupied Greece; in this way the equilibrium will be re-established.'
>
> ### *Galeazzo Ciano, from a diary entry for 12 October 1940*

The invasion of Greece was poorly planned and incompetently led. When it stalled, Hitler came to the rescue with a successful invasion of Yugoslavia and Greece in April 1941. In the following month, Italy lost its East African empire of Eritrea, Somalia and Abyssinia to the British and Abyssinian resistance fighters. To strengthen and recover Italy's weakening hold on Libya, Hitler sent in the brilliant general, Erwin Rommel. Arguably, the diversion of German resources to assist Italy in the Balkans and North Africa contributed to Hitler's downfall too.

FURTHER SETBACKS

Meanwhile, the British navy had badly mauled the Italian fleet in an attack at Taranto on 11–12 November 1940, gaining temporary control of the Mediterranean. The subsequent Battle of Matapan in March 1941 had finally wrecked Mussolini's aim of winning control of the Mediterranean. Fearful that Hitler now found little to choose between Vichy France, Spain or Italy as effective European allies, Mussolini was determined to demonstrate that Italy was still Germany's senior partner. This resulted in two further errors of judgement. He sent 227 000 Italian troops to support Hitler's invasion of Russia after June 1941, together with equipment and vehicles that were sorely needed in North Africa. Then, on 7 December 1941, he joined Germany in declaring war on the USA, following Japan's attack on Pearl Harbor.

'With Hitler trapped on the Eastern Front, Mussolini sinks like a stone'
A Russian view of Mussolini's downfall

War against Greece [?]

'Hitler was later to claim that Mussolini's declaration of war against Greece lost him the war, because with the increasing disasters of the Italian forces in Greece, the Germans had to go to the assistance of the Italians, and thus postpone the invasion of Russia ... From this moment, Italy had lost the war...'

A. J. P. Taylor, The War Lords (Penguin, 1976)

To what extent does A. J. P. Taylor's conclusion in the above quotation support the point made in the Russian cartoon?

Analysis of sources

- Explain the Russian cartoon opposite.
- Judge whether the point that the cartoon makes is a complete explanation of Mussolini's downfall.

THE KEY ISSUES

- Why did the king dismiss Mussolini on 25 July 1943?
- Why was Mussolini unable to revive popular support for Fascism in the Republic of Salò?

THE KEY SKILLS

Analysis of causation
Interpretation

WHAT YOU HAVE TO DO

Explain why those who had kept Mussolini in power lost confidence in him. Explain why Mussolini's Italian Social Republic did not win popular support.

Loss of confidence

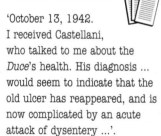

'October 13, 1942.
I received Castellani, who talked to me about the *Duce*'s health. His diagnosis ... would seem to indicate that the old ulcer has reappeared, and is now complicated by an acute attack of dysentery ...'.

'October 23, 1942. ... I see Farinacci and Bottai. They are both exasperated by the internal situation, which is aggravated by the absolute inadequacy of the Party. There is much talk about a report by the provincial secretaries of the Fascist Party of a meeting ... during which the "Petacci affair" was officially discussed ...'

Galeazzo Ciano, from diary entries, 1939–1943

Mussolini's Downfall

POPULAR DISCONTENT

Mussolini's power had depended upon the combined support or tolerance of the monarchy, the Church, industrialists, the army and the *ras*. His popularity with the Italian people depended on maintaining internal stability and winning prestige for Italy abroad. Little by little, Mussolini lost this support. The principal cause was the alliance with Germany, which King Victor Emmanuele had never liked and which the Church blamed for the introduction of racial laws in 1938. Soon, Germany was taking from Italy more than it gave in coal and iron. Half of the 350 000 Italian workers sent to Germany were skilled. Agricultural produce sent to Germany made worse the shortages already brought about by poor distribution and incomplete rationing. When farmers realised that the system of centrally stockpiling produce was being incompetently and corruptly managed, they began to cheat and hold back produce to sell on the black market.

Inadequate anti-aircraft defences exposed Italy's industrial cities to the full brunt of Allied bombings. These intensified in the second half of 1942, destroying factories, disrupting production, and causing homelessness and mass evacuations to rural areas. Efforts to recover and maintain essential wartime supplies led to longer working hours and tighter factory discipline. Disaffection spread to all classes. An indication of a loss of confidence in the regime was the decline from 1942 in the purchase by middle-class savers of Treasury Bonds, which was the government's main method of borrowing money, apart from raising taxes.

Allied landings in North Africa in November 1942 marked the turning-point in the war. In March 1943, the first great strikes since the Fascists came to power took place. The inability of the Fascist Party to stem disaffection meant that the Fascists had outlived their usefulness to the industrialists. The loss of Libya in May 1943, and the invasion of Italy itself in July along with the first bombing of Rome, meant that Mussolini's days in power were numbered. His health had broken down again. What popularity he had left was squandered by favours to the corrupt relatives of his mistress Clara Petacci.

COUP

The sacking and replacement of military leaders such as Badoglio and Admiral Cavagnari in 1940 had not paid off. The demotion of Ciano, Bottai and Grandi between February and April was now repaid by their disloyalty. They formed one of two groups who pressed for a meeting of the Grand Council. The other group, led by Farinacci and the new Fascist Party Secretary, Scorza, wanted even closer co-operation with Nazi Germany. Before the meeting took place, Mussolini met Hitler at Feltre on 19 July. He promised to inform the *Führer* of Italy's need for peace, but his courage failed him.

The Grand Council met on 24 July. They voted 19 to 7 in favour of a motion by Grandi that, as they no longer had confidence in

Mussolini, full powers should be restored to the king. On 25 July, at 5 p.m., the king dismissed Mussolini and had him arrested.

THE REPUBLIC OF SALÒ

Marshal Badoglio replaced Mussolini as head of state. He negotiated Italy's surrender on 8 September 1943. Four days later, in a daring commando raid, the Germans rescued Mussolini from his mountain prison at Gran Sasso and installed him as head of a new Fascist regime in the far north of Italy. Mussolini called this the Italian Social Republic, but it became known as the Republic of Salò. German doctors nursed Mussolini back to health.

The Italian Social Republic was little more than a puppet regime under the supervision of German Ambassador Rahn and SS General Wolff. The Germans occupied most of Italy's northeastern provinces, and ruled them directly as part of the Greater German Reich. The *Gestapo* brutally persecuted the small community of Italian Jews and conscripted thousands of Italian men, who were sent to Germany as forced labour.

Mussolini, although burnt out and reluctant to resume his duties as *Duce*, sought to reshape his vision of Fascism and rally support. He reverted to some of the early radicalism of the 1919 Fascist programme. There was a strong socialist element. Socialisation replaced corporativism: it was a cross between nationalisation and workers' control of industry. Mussolini was now fiercely anti-monarchist and anti-Semitic. However, since the Republic was in one of the most Catholic regions of Italy, he was tolerant of the Church. A number of other Fascist exiles who had sought German protection joined Mussolini. They included Farinacci, Pavolini, Buffarini-Guidi and Preziosi. The Germans observed with contempt their intrigues and squabbles. Those Fascists who had betrayed Mussolini in July and who had the misfortune to be captured were put on trial and executed. They included his son-in-law, Ciano.

MUSSOLINI'S DEATH

Meanwhile, Italians in growing numbers joined the resistance movement. By August 1944 the Allies reached Florence and, in early 1945, helped the Resistance to liberate northern Italy. The game was up. Mussolini attempted to negotiate with the Resistance but, sensing danger, fled northwards with other Italian ministers under the protection of a German unit. The Resistance stopped them at Dongo and recognised Mussolini, despite a feeble attempt to disguise himself in a *Luftwaffe* greatcoat and helmet. They took the ministers to the nearest town and shot them. Mussolini, being a bigger fish, was held prisoner for a while in a farm building where his mistress, Clara Petacci, joined him. A communist leader of the Resistance, 'Colonel Valerio', then took them away the next morning, and shot them on the afternoon of 28 April 1945. Mussolini was 61. On the next day their corpses – together with those of Farinacci, Starace, Bombacci, Pavolini and Buffarini – were strung up by the heels in the Piazzale Loreto at Milan on public display.

The corpses of Mussolini, his mistress and other Fascist leaders

A palingenetic form of populist ultra-nationalism – this definition of Fascism can be broken up and literally translated as follows:

- *palin* – again, anew
- *genesis* – creation, birth
- *populist* – political forces that depend on 'people power'; ideas and policies that pander to the prejudices of a population
- *ultra* – something that affects all and reaches beyond; extremes; dynamic
- *nationalism* – unity and intense pride in the shared identity of a people within territorial boundaries and in independence from foreign rule

Fascism as an Ideology

IDEOLOGICAL DEFINITIONS

Until the 1990s, a typical textbook view of Fascism was that it lacked a coherent ideology:

'Fascism never presented any real ideological coherence. It was in large measure the projection on a public screen of the monstrous, semi-comic, gesticulating figure of Mussolini. Just this also kept it from the vileness of Nazism. Fascist rule was important in Italian foreign policy, yet effected no substantial changes at home. This may be related to the lack of positive content in Fascism.'
J. M. Roberts, Europe 1880–1945 (Longman, 2nd edn, 1989)

Unlike communism, which offered a systematic and rational body of thought to guide action, Fascism appeared to be largely an improvised and opportunist reaction. Fascism seemed to invent itself as it went along, changing and redefining itself in the process. Thus, much of the original 1919 programme which launched the Fascist movement was abandoned by the time an official definition by Mussolini himself appeared in the Italian Encyclopedia of 1932. As he explained:

'The years which preceded the March on Rome were ones in which the overriding need for action did not allow us the possibility of profound philosophical enquiries or complete doctrinal elaborations.' **Enciclopedia Italiana, 1932**

Writing in 1923, one Fascist shrewdly commented:

'There is no Fascist political doctrine other than the concept of the Nation hierarchically organised … and this is revealed by the multiplicity of interpretations made by Fascists themselves so that each individual believes in his own type of Fascism.'
Augusto De Marsanich, Critica Fascista, 15 December 1923

Such apparent diversity rather than coherence has made it easier for historians to describe the common characteristics of Fascism at different stages of its development rather than find a convincing definition of its ideological core. Nevertheless, there have been attempts to provide such a definition. In his book *The Nature of Fascism*, Roger Griffin combines the idea of 'rebirth' with political forces driven by 'people power', which produce a form of radical nationalism that 'goes beyond and hence rejects anything compatible with liberal institutions' or traditions of rational thought since the late 18th century. Put concisely, Fascism is 'a palingenetic form of populist ultra-nationalism'.

Roger Eatwell, on the other hand, defines Fascism as seeking a different political system from liberal capitalism or communism:

'Fascist ideology is, therefore, a form of thought which preaches the need for social rebirth in order to forge a holistic–national radical Third Way. This is a formulation which clearly excludes many alleged examples of Fascism, such as the essentially conservative dictatorship of General Franco in Spain. Yet it is flexible enough to include different varieties of Fascism, for instance the biologically-based nationalism of the Nazis and the culturally-based Italian Fascism.' **Roger Eatwell, Fascism, a History, 1996**

See Roger Eatwell, Fascism, a History (Vintage, 1996) and Roger Griffin, The Nature of Fascism (Routledge, 1991).

THE CHARACTERISTICS OF ITALIAN FASCISM

The characteristics of Italian Fascism were broadly that it was ultra-nationalist and, in the end, racist. It became a mass movement, the unity of which depended upon the charismatic and authoritarian leadership of Mussolini. It sought the reconciliation of the interests of both workers and capitalists in a Corporative State in order to achieve autarky. Above all, Mussolini wanted Italy to be 'great, respected and feared'. To achieve this, he wanted Italians to breed a nation of warriors and acquire an empire.

Fascism began as an 'anti-movement' – anti-capitalist, anti-democratic, anti-liberal, anti-socialist, anti-monarchist and anti-clerical. Fascists who supported the first manifesto of 1919 were also strongly against all forms of dictatorship, whether of the sword or of the cocked hat, of money or of numbers. 'We will accept only one dictatorship, that of will and intelligence,' stated the *Fascist Manifesto* of 1919.

En route to power, the Fascists became the strike-breaking allies of industrialists and landowners, participated in elections, flirted with all the political parties, made a temporary electoral alliance with Giolitti's Liberal Party, and abandoned their anti-monarchism. In his first speech as a newly elected member of the Italian Parliament in 1921, Mussolini spoke on the conflict between Arabs and Jews in Palestine, and said:

> 'No one should read into my words any hint of anti-Semitism, which would be a new thing in this Chamber. I recognise that the sacrifice of blood on the part of Italian Jews during the war was great and generous.' *From Opera Omnia, XVI, 1957, page 439*

In power, Mussolini established an authoritarian regime and sought good relations with the Church. In 1938, he introduced racial laws that discriminated against the Jews.

Fascism underwent its most intensive period of ideological development from the late 1920s. The key features of this development were the concepts of totalitarianism, the Corporative State and autarky. Although not achieved as intended, in practice considerable effort was invested in the attempt to do so. The practical reality was that the Fascist regime was sustained in power by a consensus of the monarchy, the Church, industrialists and the armed forces. This meant that compromises were necessary. Friendship with Germany, and dependence on the latter for coal and iron, led to the breakdown of this consensus and the overthrow of Mussolini. Installed by the Germans as a puppet dictator of the Republic of Salò in 1943, Mussolini reverted to the anti-monarchism of the 1919 Fascist programme, retained the anti-Semitism acquired in the 1930s and promoted the concept of 'socialisation' (adapted from 'corporativism').

Fascism was violent and glorified war. According to Mussolini, 'Violence, to be effective, must be surgical, intelligent and chivalrous' (3 January 1925). He wrote:

> 'War alone brings up to their highest tension all human energies and puts the stamp of nobility upon the peoples who have the courage to meet it …'. *From The Doctrine of Fascism, 1932*

Charismatic – possessing an attractive aura that inspires a following or enthuses people: a spellbinding quality that makes an individual the focus of attention, or makes people aware of his or her presence

Mussolini's survival in power

Mussolini was in power for 21 years. What is your view on each of the following statements?

- Mussolini was consistent in his beliefs.
- The secret of Mussolini's survival was his ability to adapt and change Fascist ideology.
- Ideology was crucial to the length of time Mussolini was in power.
- The coherence of Fascism depended upon the charismatic leadership of Mussolini.

Fascism and Other Ideologies

THE KEY ISSUES

- How did Fascism in Italy compare with Fascism in Germany?
- How did Fascism compare with communism in the Soviet Union?

THE KEY SKILLS

Comparison and analysis

WHAT YOU HAVE TO DO

Identify the similarities and differences between Italian Fascism and National Socialism, and between Italian Fascism and Soviet communism.

Aryan – in Nazi ideology, this meant a non-Jewish white person of north European descent, who possessed the biological qualifications to belong to the 'master race'

Race and racism ?

'The concept of race is a purely biological concept. It is therefore based on factors other than the concept of the people or the nation, based essentially on historic, linguistic and religious considerations ... The population of present day Italy is of Aryan origin.'

From The Manifesto of Racist Scientists, 14 July 1938

What evidence is there that this explanation was the result of German influence?

SIMILARITIES WITH NAZISM

Fascism in Italy and Nazism had in common the aim of national regeneration – a form of rebirth. Two charismatic and authoritarian leaders, Hitler and Mussolini, inspired popular support. Both movements were ultra-nationalist and made common enemies of liberalism and communism. There were similarities of style, especially in the wearing of uniforms, and the love of parades and of massed crowds. Both Italian Fascists and Nazis found modern technology – especially to do with speed or war – exhilarating. They took advantage of the new technologies of the radio and cinema for propaganda.

Despite their admiration for technology, they were both conservative in their attitude towards 'modernism', especially if associated with living in towns and cities. They romanticised the values of rural life. Their conservatism extended to the role of women, who were idealised as home-makers and mothers. Both movements were revolutionary until tamed by being established in power. Despite setting out as enemies of big business, both enlisted the support of landowners and industrialists. Italian Fascism and Nazism aimed at autarky, and sought room for expansion – *spazio vitale* or *Lebensraum* – through conquest of territory.

DIFFERENCES FROM NAZISM

Italian Fascism and Nazism were closer in theory than in practice. In this, racism is a grey area. Although Mussolini later claimed he had always been an anti-Semite, he often used to ridicule the racial theories of Nazis as 'unscientific' and 'ridiculous'. The feeling that racism was un-Italian was a widespread sentiment. Italian reaction to the introduction of racial laws in 1938 was that, by and large, they were products of German influence in the same way as the *passo romano* (German goose-step). The ideology of National Socialism was biologically based from the outset. Hitler's biography, *Mein Kampf* (1924), provided a clear statement of his ideological convictions. His anti-Semitism sprang from a conspiracy theory about Jewish aspirations for world domination. Mussolini never expressed such paranoia. The nationalism of Italian Fascism was culturally based. It was rooted in the glorious past of the Roman Empire – a vision referred to, and embellished, as *Romanità*.

In practice, Mussolini did not achieve power on the scale of Hitler in order to realise his vision of a totalitarian state. Whereas Mussolini had to contend with the constitutional obstacle of the monarchy and the rival influence of the Catholic Church, Hitler had no such obstacles after 1934. Partly for this reason, the image of Italian Fascism seems more benign and tolerant than that of Nazi Germany. The scale of arrests and imprisonments for political crimes was not as great in Italy and, on the whole, the treatment of political prisoners was less brutal. Even the persecution of Jews in Italy after 1938 lacked the thoroughness and commitment exhibited by the Nazis. Cultural oppression in Italy did not reach the same heights as in Germany, where there were organised book-burnings and persecution of artists whose work was thought degenerate. In general, Fascist Italy was more tolerant of intellectuals and artists.

SIMILARITIES WITH MARXISM–LENINISM AND STALINISM

Up to 1919, Mussolini was a socialist, despite his ejection from the Italian Socialist Party (the PSI) in 1914. One biographer, Denis Mack Smith, believes that at the end of his life Mussolini reverted to the socialism of his youth. Like the Russian revolutionary, Lenin, he saw liberal democracy as an enemy and believed in the need for dedicated, full-time activists who would lead the masses. On 9 January 1910, he said:

> 'Socialist workers must form the vanguard, vigilant and combative, that spurs the mass never to forget the vision of the ideal goal.'

The Fascist movement launched by Mussolini in 1919 was as revolutionary in word and manner as the Bolsheviks led by Lenin. Both saw war as a means of radicalising the masses. Lenin's legacy to Stalin was a one-party dictatorship, which he transformed more ruthlessly and efficiently than either Mussolini or Hitler into a totalitarian regime. The historian, Richard Pipes, has made this comparison:

> 'At bottom the totalitarian regimes of the left and the right varieties were united not only by similar political philosophies and practices, but by the common psychology of their founders: its driving motive was hatred and its expression violence. Mussolini, the frankest of them all, referred to violence as a "moral therapeutic" because it forced people to make clear commitments.'
> ### *Richard Pipes, Russia under the Bolshevik Regime, 1919–1924*
> ### *(Harvill, 1994)*

Stalin encouraged the cult of personality as shamelessly as Mussolini. His policy of 'socialism in one country' represented not just a pragmatic break with the international socialism of Lenin and Trotsky, but an appeal to nationalist instincts. Mussolini praised him for turning into a 'secret Fascist'.

DIFFERENCES FROM MARXISM–LENINISM AND STALINISM

Stalin was the architect of an empire, the size of which was beyond Mussolini's wildest dreams. It was founded on the principles of Marxism–Leninism, which replaced capitalism with a highly centralised command economy. Italian Fascism compromised, and in the end sided, with landowners and industrialists at the expense of the workers. The achievements of Stalin's Five-Year Plans were genuine and impressive compared with those of the Corporative State – despite the human cost. Stalin's regime ruthlessly purged millions of dissidents, exterminated their leaders and enslaved their followers in labour camps. It indulged in cultural and religious oppression which exceeded that of the Nazis, whose own excesses discomforted the Italians. Stalin came closer to achieving a totalitarian state than either Mussolini or Hitler.

The fasces
The Fascist emblem, a symbol of authority adopted from Ancient Rome

See Richard Pipes, *Russia under the Bolshevik Regime, 1919–1924* (Harvill, 1994). Richard Pipes is Polish by birth. From 1950 he taught at Harvard in the USA, where he became Professor of History. He is a specialist in the history of 19th- and 20th-century Russia. He writes from a perspective which is wholly unsympathetic to Lenin and his successors. From 1981 to 1982, he served on President Ronald Reagan's National Security Council as Director of Soviet and East European Affairs.

Totalitarianism ?

Decide whether you agree or disagree with Richard Pipes' statements that 'the totalitarian regimes had similar political philosophies' and that their founders had a 'common psychology'.

What is synthesis?

Synthesis is the bringing together of sources of information and points of view. It is an attempt to create one whole picture from fragments and different perspectives.

How is synthesis different from narrative?

Narrative is an outline of events, told as a story. The process of producing an outline is a form of synthesis, but not to an advanced level. Synthesis at A-level addresses Key Issues. In doing so, synthesis draws together arguments about, and interpretations of, events to make propositions or conclusions. The status of these propositions or conclusions is hypothetical; that is to say, they are theories to be proved or disproved by reference to facts.

Test the hypothesis

Were opportunism, violence and blackmail the key ingredients in Mussolini's rise to power?

Synthesis *(Establishing a Hypothesis)*

1. WHAT WAS THE IMPACT OF THE FIRST WORLD WAR ON ITALY?

On the one hand, the First World War did little to solve – and indeed intensified – the economic, political and social divisions within Italy. A gulf remained between the relatively backward economy of southern Italy and the industrialised and agriculturally more prosperous economy of the north. There were still low levels of literacy. Tension still existed between the Church and state. Lack of faith in the politicians who governed Italy was still widespread, and Italy still lacked the great power status that it had hoped to gain from the war.

On the other hand, Italy emerged from the First World War on the winning side, with raised expectations after the sacrifices made in human and material resources. These expectations were fuelled by the extension of democracy, promises of land reform and from the unrest during the years 1919–1920 caused by the rising tide of socialism.

2. HOW DID MUSSOLINI COME TO POWER IN 1922?

Mussolini created a new movement, Fascism, which reflected disillusionment with the conventional political parties. It attracted support from disgruntled extremists from virtually all political perspectives. The Fascists were united by nationalism and by their anger and disappointment over the peace settlements. They benefited from the eclipse of the charismatic nationalist rebel, D'Annunzio, and from the unrest during the years 1919–1920 caused by the rising tide of socialism.

Fascism became a mass movement by abandoning much of its original political programme, and also by putting its Blackshirt squads at the disposal of landowners and industrialists in order to end the intimidation of peasants and workers by the Catholic peasant leagues and socialist trades unions, and in order to break up strikes. In this way, Fascist local leaders, called *ras*, took control of the northern provinces. And Mussolini took advantage of rivalry between the *ras* to maintain his position as their leader. At the same time, the Fascists benefited from the divisions among their political opponents and rivals, even flirting with the possibility of alliances in order to play one off against the other. One consequence of this was an electoral alliance with Giolitti's liberals in May 1921, from which the Fascists not only gained 35 seats in Parliament but also respectability and credibility.

By 1922, the Fascists had enough regional power to make a direct bid for government. Fear of an internal palace coup by his pro-Fascist cousin, awareness that the support of the army could not be taken for granted, and knowledge that leading politicians, landowners, industrialists, newspaper owners and the Church all favoured accommodation rather than confrontation – all of these factors prompted the king to take the initiative. He abandoned the advice of his Prime Minster, Facta, to have a showdown, allowed his rival Salandra an opportunity to attempt (without success) to form a government that would include Fascists, and then offered the job of Prime Minister to Mussolini.

3. Why did Mussolini Become a Dictator?

Mussolini intended to be a dictator. His government was developing into a dictatorship well before the Matteotti crisis of 1924. From the start, Mussolini intimidated the divided opposition into giving his government a vote of confidence and granting it emergency powers for economic and administrative reforms. Normal government decision-making by the Council of Ministers was bypassed by the setting up of the Fascist Grand Council where, in effect, Mussolini was the real decision-maker. The creation of the Fascist Militia and a secret hit squad, or *cheka*, to terrorise outspoken opponents provided the means of imposing a one-party dictatorship as soon as the moment was ripe.

Meanwhile, Mussolini went through the motions of legality. This was in part to avoid uniting, and thereby creating, an effective opposition. It was also for the sake of appearances, in order to maintain the tacit support of the monarchy, the landowners and industrialists, and the Pope. In an atmosphere of threat and intimidation, however, he ensured the passing of a new electoral law to give two-thirds of the seats in Parliament to any party that gained 25% of the vote. Both before and during the elections that followed, opposition leaders suffered harassment and physical violence. Fascist thugs disrupted normal voting procedures. The murder of Matteotti for speaking out against these outrages was a watershed, but not the immediate cause of creating a one-party dictatorship.

It is true that evidence brought to the attention of the king, which implicated Fascists in other acts of murder and violence, caused the *ras* to threaten to depose Mussolini as their leader unless he set up a full dictatorship. However, this turn of events merely served to help Mussolini to recover a temporary loss of nerve. In any case, it was rather like kicking at an open door. Because they had withdrawn from Parliament in protest, the king had refused to back the demands of opposition leaders to sack Mussolini, and the Pope had disassociated himself from Catholics who supported them.

4. What was the True Nature of Mussolini's Dictatorship from 1925 to 1928?

From 1925 to 1928, Mussolini aimed at the creation of a totalitarian state. He did succeed in creating an authoritarian regime during this period, but one which, arguably, was neither truly Fascist nor totalitarian. The senior personnel who ran the government departments and police tended to be career civil servants rather than political appointees. This was compounded by the fact that the nominal head of eight of the ministries was Mussolini himself.

During this time, Mussolini tamed the revolutionary nature of the Fascist movement by subordinating its organisation under his personal control and removing potential rivals from positions of power. Meanwhile, to offset the repression of independent organisations, and in an attempt to popularise the regime, the government sponsored organisations aimed at capturing the hearts and minds of both the young (ONB and GUF) and adults (*Dopolavoro*).

Test the hypothesis ?

To what extent does the evidence support the following view?

'Mussolini survived resistance to the creation of a dictatorship, despite the Matteotti crisis, not just because opposition was weak and divided, but also because there was a consensus of support for an authoritarian regime.

'This consensus (in other words, general acceptance) was based upon tolerance – if not support – from landowners, industrialists, the king, the Pope, the leaders of the armed forces and the middle classes. The basic reason for this was that Mussolini brought about stability, and law and order, after years of instability, lawlessness and weak governments.

'In the first years of his dictatorship, Mussolini sought to consolidate his power, rather than risk upsetting this consensus. For this reason, he did not ensure that "fascistisation" took place at every level of government and in every institution.'

Choosing between hypotheses

In addition to the need to test hypothetical propositions and conclusions individually, it is also necessary to know how to choose between two hypotheses. The process involves the use of supporting evidence for one hypothesis in order to challenge the other, and vice versa. A conclusion is then reached as to which is the more convincing.

Which is the more convincing hypothesis?

A. J. P. Taylor and Denis Mack Smith provide examples of two historians who highlight the semi-comic, showman qualities of Mussolini. They draw attention to his opportunism and inconsistencies.

Their entertaining hypothesis is that Mussolini was a charismatic speaker with a journalist's flair for eye-catching headlines; he had an instinct for opportunity and a genius for timing. Once in power, he was a poseur who became a victim of his own propaganda. The regime that he created was more façade than substance.

An alternative hypothesis is that Mussolini would not have survived in power for so long had he not been an astute politician with a clear vision of what he wanted to achieve. Fascism provided a rationale for policy which turned his regime into something more than a repressive dictatorship.

5. Did the Fascist Regime Develop into More than a Repressive Dictatorship?

On balance, the Fascist regime developed into something more than a repressive dictatorship, but less than a totalitarian one. Mussolini's well-publicised 'battles' – to make Italy self-sufficient in food, to increase the value of the lira, to increase the birth rate, and to reclaim land by draining marshes – had more to do with prestige and plans to acquire an empire than with Fascism. Similarly, reconciliation with the Church through the Lateran Treaties of 1929 aimed at gaining prestige for, and popularising, the dictatorship. Significantly, they did not end the rivalry between Catholic youth and Fascist organisations.

The management of the economy through corporations that represented workers and employers seemed to offer the prospect of a 'Third Way' to ensure harmonious industrial relations – without following the paths of communism or liberal capitalism. In reality, it amounted to little more than an exercise in bureaucracy and propaganda, which benefited employers more than workers. During the Depression, almost all economic policy decisions bypassed the corporations.

However, it was during these years that efforts to indoctrinate Italians with Fascist ideals intensified through education, youth organisations, culture and propaganda. Hero worship of Mussolini and the cult of *Il Duce* reached new heights. The party expanded its membership and the number of capillary organisations in order to incorporate the masses and extend its network of surveillance and control. Government intervention ensured that the effects of the Depression in Italy, though serious, were less severe than in other western European countries. However, despite all these efforts, Mussolini frequently despaired of making Italians Fascists in his own image. He saw war as a necessary means of toughening them up to achieve this.

6. Did Mussolini Follow a Consistent Plan in Foreign Policy between 1922 and 1935?

Mussolini wanted Italy to be 'great, respected and feared'. He was driven by ambition to create an empire. His domestic policies were consistent with expansionist aims. In striving for autarky (economic self-sufficiency), he used the language of 'battle'. Through propaganda slogans and images, and through the curriculum of the youth organisation (ONB), he emphasised preparation for war. There was considerable investment in the armed forces and industries linked to war.

The Corfu affair of 1923, the negotiated acquisition of Fiume in 1924, and the role played by Mussolini in the Locarno agreement of 1925 served to earn prestige for Italy and assert its position as a Mediterranean power. Meanwhile, Mussolini intrigued to undermine the stability of the postwar peace settlements, especially in southeastern Europe. He provided weapons and training facilities for terrorists and dissident paramilitary organisations in Hungary, Bulgaria and Yugoslavia. He attempted to develop client relationships with Albania and Abyssinia, in order to make them economically dependent upon Italy.

7. WHY WAS ITALY'S INVASION OF ABYSSINIA A TURNING-POINT?

Mussolini reached the height of his popularity in Italy by conquering Abyssinia; but his subsequent involvement of Italy in the Spanish Civil War and in a closer relationship with Germany led to his downfall.

The occupation of Abyssinia challenged the authority of the League of Nations, obliging its senior members, Britain and France, to apply sanctions. Although they did so half-heartedly – and behind the scenes negotiated concessions in the Horn of Africa – they failed to prevent a bonding between Mussolini and Hitler. Intoxicated with success in Abyssinia, Mussolini aspired to forge a new Fascist order in Europe. For this reason, he invested more resources than Italy could afford to assist Franco in Spain against the Republican government and its socialist allies. He paid a heavy price diplomatically – not least because of Italian attacks on British, French, Greek and Danish cargo ships.

Domestically, there were ominous signs that the popularity of the regime was waning. To the disquiet of many Italians, Mussolini abandoned Italy's traditional defence of Austrian independence against a political union (*Anschluss*) with Germany, forbidden under the terms of the peace settlement. The Nazi invasion of Austria in 1938, the introduction of racist laws and other signs of German influence began to break the consensus of tacit support for the regime by the king and the Church. A formal alliance with Germany in May 1939 led to the ultimate disaster – a war for which Italy was ill-prepared.

8. WAS MUSSOLINI TO BLAME FOR HIS OWN DOWNFALL?

Despite the initial delaying of Italy's entry into the Second World War, Mussolini could not be convinced, by the best advice available to him, to stay out of the conflict permanently. Even then, his insistence on fighting a 'parallel war', compounded by errors of judgement, lost Italy – and, arguably, Germany – the war. Military failures and deprivations on the home front through mismanagement of rationing, and commitments to supply food resources and Italian labour to Germany, fuelled discontent. Inadequate anti-aircraft defences and Allied bombardment of industrial cities, culminating in the bombing of Rome itself, shattered remaining confidence in the *Duce*.

Finally, the alienation of his closest supporters among the Fascist leaders brought about his dismissal by the king. Although rescued from imprisonment by the Nazis, Mussolini could offer little to rally popular support. Installed as dictator of the so-called Italian Social Republic in northern Italy, he was no more than a puppet of the Germans and was fated to suffer a grisly end at the hands of Italian partisans.

Test the hypothesis ?

Begin by making a critical comparison and analysis of the following two hypotheses:

1 Mussolini was driven by his ambition for empire, which he saw as the key to making Italy a great power. To achieve this ambition, he risked diplomatic isolation by carrying out the conquest of Abyssinia and by forging an unpopular alliance with Germany. However, the consequence was a breakdown of the consensus which kept Mussolini in power, leading to his downfall.

2 Mussolini had no clear plan to make Italy 'great, respected and feared', other than to stir up trouble in order to undermine the peace settlements. He gambled, with inadequate military resources, on the weak resolve of Britain and France to stand up to Italian and German aggression. The decision in 1940 to honour Italy's military alliance with Germany contributed to Germany's defeat and caused his own downfall.

Now, using what you have judged to be the valid parts of the propositions, construct a hypothesis of your own.

Essay planning

One useful strategy for essay planning is to begin by responding to the written question with a hypothesis (in other words, a conclusion in answer to the question). Then, this hypothesis can be broken down into its main parts in order to provide the different sections of the essay. In each of these sections, the relevant part of the hypothesis is supported by evidence in order to build up the overall argument of the essay.

What is meant by the term 'argument' at A-level?

Historians set out to discover the truth about what happened in the past. They have to convince themselves and others that what they find out is the truth. This means that they have to use evidence in different ways in order to establish what really happened and why it happened, and in order to convince an audience that it is the truth.

The skills required include:

- interrogating evidence by asking the right questions
- assessing the quality of the evidence
- making informed guesses where there are gaps
- marshalling different points of view
- creating a logical structure for presentation

At its best, 'argument' examines and discusses all possible answers to a question, and persuades the audience that the conclusion reached is the correct one.

Argument

1. QUESTIONS ABOUT MUSSOLINI'S RISE TO POWER

(a) 'The twin myths of the mutilated victory and the Bolshevik threat pushed Italy towards fascism.' How far is this a complete assessment of the factors that brought Mussolini to power?

Essay plan

The 'twin myths' are insufficient alone to explain the rise of Fascism. However, they are factors which need to be considered: Italians felt cheated of promises made in the Treaty of London of 1915, and the 'two red years' of 1919–1920 gave the Fascists an opportunity to exploit fears of a socialist revolution.

Other factors to consider include: problems unsolved by intervention in the war; the failure of governments to solve these; the effects of proportional representation in producing unstable governments; the eclipse of D'Annunzio; the role of Mussolini; tactical alliances, for example with Giolitti; the use of *squadristi* to break up illegal land occupation and strikes; lawlessness; weak and divided opposition; the attitude of the Pope towards the *Popolari*; the Fascists' takeover in the northern provinces, led by *ras*; and the role of the king when faced with the March on Rome.

Commentary

An essay needs an introduction that immediately addresses the question, followed by a development section that elaborates and critically analyses the key points of the introduction, and a conclusion. The above plan could be redrafted into an introduction and then each 'factor' elaborated upon and examined in the development section of the essay. Note that one valued strategy is to state the 'answer', or line of argument, immediately. This should emerge again in the conclusion, ideally with an alternative view that takes into account an assessment of other factors.

(b) Why, in the period 1922–1925, was there so little effective opposition to the Fascist takeover of the Italian state?

Essay plan

The Nationalists were absorbed into the Fascist Party; the Socialist Party, the liberals and the conservatives were divided; and the Pope undermined the leadership of the Catholic *Popolari*. All were intimidated by the veiled threat of a Fascist takeover.

Other explanations include: the initial appearance of moderation and continuity in the formation of a 'national' coalition government; the imposition of law and order after years of unrest; the apparently legal changing of the electoral system in 1923; Farinacci's ruthless taming of the Fascist Party; and *squadristi* and *cheka* violence.

Mussolini survived the Matteotti crisis because of the tactical errors of the Aventine Secession and a consensus of support from the king, industrialists, landowners, the Church, the armed forces and newspaper owners.

Commentary

This essay requires an examination of the weaknesses of the opposition, the role and tactics of the Fascists, and the nature of support for the Fascists.

2. QUESTIONS ABOUT MUSSOLINI'S DICTATORSHIP

Source 1

'If Fascism has been a criminal plot, if violence has resulted from a certain historical, political and moral atmosphere, the responsibility is mine, because I have deliberately created this atmosphere.'

Benito Mussolini, from a speech to the Italian Parliament on 3 January 1925

Source 2

'Italy, if she is to count for anything in the world, must have a population of not less than 60 million inhabitants by the middle of this century.'

Benito Mussolini, from a speech to the Italian Parliament on 25 May 1927

Source 3

'In the Corporation the power of the employers and employees is balanced and reconciled.'

From *Critica Fascista*, 1934

Do these three sources tell us enough about Mussolini's methods of establishing total Fascist control? Use your knowledge to assess the extent to which they were successful.

Plan for answer

The source extracts give a partial view of Mussolini's methods and no indication as to the extent of their success. Source 1 is a response to the Matteotti crisis, which nearly toppled Mussolini's regime, while source 2 relates to the 'Battle for Births' campaign, which was only one part of a series of initiatives, all of which fell short of their goal. Arguably, Mussolini never took seriously the idea of corporations referred to in source 3.

Employers retained the upper hand over workers. Finally, the influence of the Catholic Church and the constitutional powers of the monarchy frustrated Mussolini's ambitions for total control.

Commentary

The need for 'argument' is signalled by words such as 'enough', 'assess' and 'extent'. It is good practice to refer to and examine each source separately, and show knowledge of their context, against which to assess the extent to which the methods referred to were successful.

Some key words and phrases that invite 'argument'

Account for – provide and make judgements about different possible explanations

Analyse – use knowledge to look critically at, make sense of, and identify strengths and weaknesses

Assess (also *How far?* or *To what extent?*) – look critically at evidence and interpretations, demonstrate knowledge that supports different points of view, and make judgements

Consider – demonstrate knowledge from different perspectives in order to make a judgement

Discuss – use knowledge critically to identify and explore Key Issues, where appropriate review interpretations, and reach conclusions

Examine – test hypotheses, interpretations, statements and explanations against the evidence

How successful? – test knowledge of criteria for 'success' (for example, 'aims', 'objectives' or 'intentions') against evidence of outcomes

3. QUESTIONS ABOUT MUSSOLINI'S FOREIGN POLICY

Was Mussolini's foreign policy based more on long-term calculation than on opportunism?

Essay plan

Mussolini was consistent in wanting an empire, and for Italy to be 'great, respected and feared'. He wanted Italy to replace France and Britain as the dominant power in the Mediterranean. He was consistent, too, in attempting to undermine the peace settlement of eastern Europe to gain advantage for Italy. The conquest of Abyssinia grew from long-term calculation.

However, Mussolini was an opportunist who sought short-term prestige from incidents such as the Corfu crisis and the acquisition of Fiume in 1924, or chances to play the international statesman, such as at Locarno in 1925 and Munich in 1938. He was not consistent in his ambitions for Fascism beyond Italy's borders, nor in keeping Nazi Germany at arm's length. The invasion of Abyssinia was a turning-point that led to the Rome–Berlin Axis. Mussolini miscalculated the cost of involvement in the Spanish Civil War (1936–1939) and made errors of judgement that resulted in a disastrous outcome for Italy in the Second World War.

Commentary

The history of Fascist foreign policy has undergone considerable revision, as new archive material has been uncovered. Early studies, such as those by the historians Gaetano Salvemini (1952) and Elizabeth Wiskemann (1949), argue that Mussolini's foreign policy was largely improvised, with no clear aims. The hugely influential Denis Mack Smith (1977) has sustained the view that Mussolini lacked a rational foreign policy.

The counter-argument – that from an early stage Mussolini had a clear awareness of what he wanted to achieve – took shape in the 1960s, led by the Italian historian, Ennio Di Nolfo. A particularly important study of Mussolini's foreign policy in the early 1930s is Esmonde Robertson's *Mussolini as Empire-builder: Europe and Africa, 1932–36*. He argues that Mussolini's aim was to make the Mediterranean an Italian sea.

The controversial Renzo De Felice saw Mussolini's foreign policy as an extension of his domestic policy. A key idea in his interpretation is that Mussolini sought to make Italy the decisive weight in the balance of power between Britain and Germany, even after the creation of the Rome–Berlin Axis and the Pact of Steel. Robert Mallett's study of *The Italian Navy and Fascist Expansionism 1935–40* provides fresh evidence that Mussolini's consistent and calculated aim was to expand the Italian empire, and that from 1937 he planned for an inevitable war against the British and French.

4. QUESTIONS LINKING MUSSOLINI'S DOMESTIC AND FOREIGN POLICIES

Why, and with what domestic consequences, did Italy undertake the invasion of Abyssinia?

Essay plan

The decision to invade Abyssinia was taken in 1932 when Italy was suffering the worst effects of the world Depression. It can be argued that the invasion in 1935 took place for four reasons. Mussolini had always wanted an empire; he judged that a spectacular foreign policy achievement would boost the popularity of the Fascist regime; he hoped that it would divert attention from the failures of domestic policies such as the Corporative State; and he believed that a war was needed to toughen up Italians, to make them good Fascists.

The immediate domestic consequences were that Mussolini became more popular than ever. However, the diplomatic isolation and League of Nations sanctions intensified the drive for autarky and policies of 'fascistisation' – and led to closer relations with Nazi Germany, culminating in the fateful Pact of Steel alliance of 1939.

Abyssinia had been the object of Italy's colonial ambitions since the 1870s. Mussolini could not resist the opportunity to achieve what his predecessors had failed to do, and thereby avenge the humiliating defeats at Dogali in 1887 and Adowa in 1896. The timing of the invasion was influenced by the preoccupation of Britain and France with Germany's departure from the League of Nations and rearmament.

The successful conquest of Abyssinia emboldened Mussolini and led to involvement in the Spanish Civil War. This, however, became unpopular, not least because of the cost in Italian lives and the financial burden. Of even greater consequence was that it initiated the Rome–Berlin Axis with Germany, whose growing influence on Italian domestic policy alienated Italians and upset the king and the Pope. A further consequence was the intensification of the drive for autarky following sanctions. The invasion of Abyssinia proved to be a turning-point for Mussolini's regime, both diplomatically and in domestic affairs. Its popularity reached a peak and thereafter declined.

Commentary

Questions linking domestic and foreign policies require awareness of the ideological nature of Fascism, and of the domestic policies intended to prepare the nation for an expansionist foreign policy: autarky, heavy investment in the armed forces, and indoctrination.

Account should also be taken of the international context of world economic depression and the rise of Nazi Germany. The extent to which foreign policy was an extension of domestic affairs and the influence of developments outside Italy should be explored.

How do you write a conclusion?

An argument is rather like a snake with its tail in its mouth. The conclusion brings us back to the answer that was proposed at the beginning.

Ideally, the reader or audience is led from the proposed answer, through a rigorous examination of the supporting evidence, to the final conclusion.

A good conclusion has the following ingredients:

- It flows naturally as part of the argument. It is not 'bolted on' with 'and so we can see ...'.
- It provides a satisfying finish to an argument that is entertaining.
- Where appropriate, it shows awareness of the tentative nature of the conclusion and raises further questions.
- At its best, a conclusion exhibits a spark of original thought. Alternatively, it is thought-provoking.

5. QUESTIONS ABOUT MUSSOLINI'S DOWNFALL

To what extent was the fall of Mussolini in 1943 a consequence of the long-term failures of Italian Fascism?

Essay plan

Mussolini's downfall was of his own making. He never took seriously the most original contribution of Fascism, the Corporative State. He did not use the considerable power at his disposal to bring about social and economic reforms that could have healed the divisions in Italy. He abandoned the radical programme of Fascism in order to secure the support of landowners and industrialists.

Under his leadership, Italy survived the world's economic depression. His personal position as *Duce* was never more popular than after the successful conquest of Abyssinia in 1936. Thereafter, he squandered his popularity by committing Italy to involvement in the Spanish Civil War and by embarking on closer relations with Nazi Germany. The latter, in particular, was distasteful to the king, who retained the constitutional power to dismiss Mussolini – which he did in 1943.

Had Mussolini chosen not to honour his Pact of Steel alliance made with Germany in 1939, his dictatorship might have survived, like Stalin's in Russia or Franco's in Spain. Arguably, Mussolini fell victim to his own propaganda and overestimated the extent to which Italy was prepared for war.

On the other hand, Mussolini was driven by his ambition to make the Mediterranean an Italian sea and his hunger for an empire which, unlike Abyssinia, would make Italy economically self-sufficient. Finally, his decision to fight a 'parallel war' alongside Hitler, rather than coordinate military operations with Germany, contributed to his downfall.

Commentary

Questions about Mussolini's downfall tend to be of three types: those which question how firmly based his rule was; those which question the success of Fascism; and those which link Mussolini's downfall with closer relations with Nazi Germany. Answers to such questions should show awareness of the issues raised by all three types of question.

Remember that the essay plans offered in this chapter are not definitive answers, but examples to illustrate possible approaches to the question. For revision purposes it would be a good idea to challenge the line of argument and try to build up your own, supported by evidence.

The important thing is to address the question with the essence of your answer straightaway, indicate your line of argument, use your knowledge, develop and support your key points with evidence – and reach a conclusion!

6. QUESTIONS ABOUT THE NATURE OF FASCISM

To what extent was the ideology of Fascism derived from the theories of Charles Darwin?

Essay plan

Fascism was derived from far more than the theories set out in Charles Darwin's *The Origin of Species*, published in 1859. An adaptation of his theory of natural selection became a popular creed towards the end of the 19th century, known as 'Social Darwinism'. Its central idea – that life is a struggle in which only the fittest survive – helped to underpin the racialist theories of Arthur de Gobineau and Houston Stewart Chamberlain. It helps to explain the title of Hitler's autobiography, *Mein Kampf* ('My Struggle').

The roots of Fascism arguably go deeper. Fascism is a fusion of reactions to the religious establishment, the 18th-century enlightenment, capitalism and the effects of industrialisation. Central to the development of Fascism were cultural nationalism, the ideas of rebirth and national regeneration, and the search for an alternative 'third-way' to liberal humanism and socialism.

Although there are similarities between the Fascisms of Mussolini and Hitler, there are distinct differences as well. The most marked difference is that Mussolini seems to have adopted anti-Semitism as a result of Nazi influence. Whereas the radical edge of Italian Fascism appears to have been derived from the influences of syndicalism, futurism and the myth of Ancient Rome (*Romanità*), Hitler's philosophy was driven at the outset by the racial theory of a 'master race' and the need for *Lebensraum*.

Another complication is that Fascism is the product of the extremism of the political left as well as of the right. Thus Stalinist Russia shared many features of the Fascist dictatorships of Italy and Germany, including Stalin's own brand of nationalism and anti-Semitism. Yet Stalinism was the legacy of Lenin's belief in 'democratic centralism' and the dictatorship of the party. As a young socialist revolutionary, Mussolini was seen by some observers as 'Italy's Lenin'. In his last days as leader of the Republic of Salò, Mussolini appears to have returned to his socialist roots.

Commentary

Questions about the nature of Fascism tend to be of three varieties: questions about the origins of Fascism; questions about the coherence of Fascism as an ideology; and questions which compare and contrast Fascism in different countries. Comparison may also extend to explaining why Fascist movements succeeded in coming to power in Italy and Germany but not in countries such as Britain and France.

How do you revise for 'argument'?

The answer to this question is the key to A-level success. Anticipate the variety of types of questions that can be asked. Looking at past questions can do this.

A good exercise, however, is to test your knowledge of the Key Issues by devising your own questions. Next, make plans of answers. A good exercise is to try to improvise the answers, first by debating them with colleagues to check for gaps in your knowledge which require further research.

A final and important type of exercise is a timed full written answer. An effective shorter version of this exercise is the 'sprint start'. For this, you practise writing the introductory paragraph or opening sentences which outline the essence of your argument.

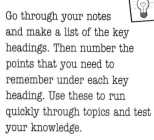
Review

1. PROGRESSION TO A-LEVEL HISTORY

The aim of this book is to assist progress from GCSE to A-level. How will you know when you have acquired a knowledge and understanding of the history of 'Mussolini and Italian Fascism' to 'Advanced Level'? One way of assessing the level of knowledge and understanding acquired is to look back at the syllabus from the examination board. In particular, you should look again at the assessment objectives of the course.

If the syllabus that you are following includes coursework, the examination board will supply outline levels of response or banding definitions used for marking. Ask your teacher, or contact the subject officer of the examination board directly, to obtain a copy. If you are going to reach Advanced Level, there should be no mystery about what they look like. Whereas the syllabus outline will make explicit the content to be assessed, levels of response will give you invaluable assistance in assessing your progress.

Another useful guide is the annual examiners' report sent by the examination boards to the colleges and schools who enter candidates for their syllabuses. The report comments on candidates' performance with a view to improving the preparation of future candidates.

2. CONTEXT, PERSPECTIVE AND KEY ISSUES

Three kinds of knowledge are needed: how the history of Italian Fascism fits into the broader context of 20th-century history; a perspective or overview of the period (see The Big Picture, pages 6–7); and relevant knowledge that is focused on the Key Issues (see pages 8–9).

General histories of Europe should be consulted to appreciate the broader context. In particular, attention is drawn to themes such as nationalism and imperialism, the impact of the First World War, the Russian revolutions of 1917, the Great Depression in the 1930s, the role of the United States of America, and the emergence of Japan in the Far East.

3. TERMINOLOGY

Understanding at A-level requires more than an ability to follow narrative and argument. A-level students should be able to demonstrate a familiarity with, and use accurately, general historical and political terminology such as 'liberalism', 'nationalism', 'capitalism', 'socialism' and 'communism'; 'radical' and 'reactionary'; 'proportional representation'; and terms that are particular to this period of Italian history, such as the *Risorgimento*, *Italia Irredente*, *trasformismo*, the 'mutilated victory', *biennio rosso*, *Dopolavoro*, the Corporative State, Fascism and 'totalitarianism'.

4. EVALUATION

Evaluation requires interrogation of primary evidence such as Mussolini's speeches, the diary of his son-in-law Ciano, propaganda and other contemporary sources. It is necessary to relate the evidence precisely to the appropriate historical context and ask questions which go beyond drawing simple inferences. For example, Mussolini's speech in which he defends his record after the murder of Matteotti needs to be read with the awareness that Mussolini's political survival was at stake, as well as examined for hints of what is to come.

A developed understanding of the usefulness and reliability of evidence is needed too. For example, although Ciano's diaries are a key source on Italian foreign policy, they are self-serving and present Ciano's role in a more flattering light than it merits. The application of A-level skills will require cross-referencing sources, handling gaps and irrelevance, and identifying problems raised by the sources for historians. What is more, the significance of evidence may change over a period of time as different questions are asked or more evidence is uncovered.

5. INTERPRETATIONS AND HISTORIOGRAPHY

It is important to know who the historians of Italian Fascism are, how their interpretations differ and why. For example, after being forced into exile in 1925, Gaetano Salvemini was one of the first Italian historians of Fascism. He exposed the reality of the Corporative State by comparing it with 'looking in a dark room for a black cat which is not there'.

Whereas histories of the period up until the mid-1960s tended to highlight the negative aspects of Fascism, controversial re-interpretation by the Italian historian, Renzo De Felice, forced other historians to take a fresh look at Fascism. De Felice portrays Fascism as a revolutionary force of the left, tamed by Mussolini while in power, and yet a threat to conservative interests until 1943.

The British historian, Denis Mack Smith, a critic of De Felice, does not take Mussolini or Fascism so seriously. However, his well-researched and entertaining biography of Mussolini has itself been criticised for being 'inclined to dismiss the *Duce* with not a little Anglo-Saxon superiority' (J. Pollard, 1998).

Both Roger Eatwell and Roger Griffin have demonstrated that Fascism as an ideology requires more serious analysis. Significant reinterpretation of Italian foreign policy in the 1930s is anticipated following greater recent access to Italian naval archives.

The nature of history

'History would be an excellent thing if only it were true.'
Leo Tolstoy, 1912

'Facts take place once and for all and cannot be recovered afterwards in their full integrity.'
David Bebbington, Patterns in History (Inter-Varsity Press, 1979)

Can you find examples from the history of Italian Fascism to support or disprove either of these statements?

History and historians

'... Before you study history, study the historian.'
E. H. Carr, What is History? (Macmillan, 1961)

'This fashion for discussing historians rather than history helps to destroy any sense ... that what they are reading about actually once happened, actually is life.'
G. R. Elton, The Practice of History (Methuen, 1967)

Examine the above quotations and decide with whom you agree most – E. H. Carr or G. R. Elton – and why.

Marx's view of history

'Men make their own history, but they do not make it just as they please; they do not make it under circumstances chosen by themselves but under circumstances directly encountered, given and transmitted from the past.'

Karl Marx, The Eighteenth Brumaire of Louis Napoleon, 1852

To what extent does your knowledge and understanding of the history of Mussolini and Fascist Italy support Marx's view of history, as outlined in the above quotation?

Namier's view of history

'History is primarily, and to a growing extent, made by man's mind and nature; but his mind does not work with the rationality that was once deemed its noblest attribute – which does not, however, mean that it necessarily works any worse ...'

Lewis Bernstein Namier (1888–1960), Personalities and Powers (Hamish Hamilton, 1955)

To what extent does Namier's judgement apply to Mussolini?

6. CAUSES, CONSEQUENCES, CHANGE AND CONTINUITY

No single factor caused the rise of Fascism and there is disagreement as to the consequences. For the first few years of the Fascist regime, many observers believe there is striking evidence of continuity with the past. Career civil servants rather than Fascists governed the provinces and dominated senior positions in the ministerial departments. Until 1925, Italy remained, in theory, a democratic country. A liberal economist managed the economy. Mussolini formed a 'national' coalition government. Throughout the Fascist period, the king retained his constitutional authority to dismiss the Prime Minister, while the Lateran Treaties left the Catholic Church independent, at times rivalling the influence of Fascist youth organisations.

From 1925, however, Mussolini created a repressive, one-party state which aimed at – but did not succeed in achieving – totalitarian control. Efforts to intensify the process of fascistisation grew in the 1930s. Mussolini's personal popularity peaked in 1935, but declined thereafter in the wake of the Spanish Civil War and closer relations between Italy and Nazi Germany.

At A-level it is important to be able to distinguish between different types of cause and consequence: those which are short-term or immediate (sometimes called 'triggers') and those which are long-term. It is often helpful to categorise them into political, economic and social causes and consequences. Any explanation of the past must take into account a variety of 'factors', ranging from the roles of individuals, political systems, resources, wars, religion, ideas – and often pure chance.

A-level students should also beware of different approaches to causation. In some cases these approaches have led to the crude labelling of historians, associating them with particular schools (or types) of history, such as 'Whig' or 'Marxist'. It is more important to understand how theories of causation have influenced approaches to the study of Italian Fascism. A 'Whiggish' analysis is likely to focus too narrowly on personalities and the anti-liberal, authoritarian nature of Fascism; Marxist perspectives, on the other hand, emphasise economic forces and social structures, interpreting Fascism as a counter-revolutionary movement that reacted to the threat of socialism.

The so-called 'Namierite' reaction to rational, ideological and schematic theories of causation is typified by attention to self-interest, inconsistencies, psychological influences and chance. Taken to extremes, this can reflect a cynical view of human behaviour which is dismissive, for example, of the motivating force of ideology and is hostile to systematic theories of causation.

7. THE IMPACT OF OTHER SUBJECT DISCIPLINES

Other subject disciplines, such as geography, economics, sociology, anthropology and politics, have had a huge influence on the methods and sources used by historians. It is now possible to form a 'bottom-up' rather than just a 'top-down' view of history. Thus, in addition to studying government papers, the public and private records of politicians, and newspapers, historians have become more aware of the value of cultural and environmental sources.

Studies of oral testimony, of climate and physical environment, of language and traditions, and of art and literature are helping to build up a picture that takes into account the perspectives of ordinary people and of local and regional variations. For example, different regional responses to Fascism are not only apparent through the study of works of literature, but also accountable through greater understanding of socio-economic and geographical circumstances.

Influenced by the approaches of the French 'Annales' school, historians now have to take into account a much wider range of sources; they can no longer concentrate simply on the actions of people in power. Since the Second World War, in particular, the methods and techniques used by social scientists have had a significant impact on historical studies. Two examples are hypothesis-testing through the use of theoretical models, and the generation and handling of data using computer technology. New methods and new sources have widened, thereby changing the nature of questions asked.

8. SIMILARITY AND DIFFERENCE

The ability to compare and contrast sources in order to establish similarities and differences is extended at A-level to include a range of criteria which make such distinctions in a variety of historical circumstances. This involves appreciating the unique nature of historical situations and showing awareness that comparison between them can be enlightening, but can also be misleading. The ability to distinguish and explain the difference between historical explanations is yet another skill acquired at A-level.

9. CONCLUSION

To find a smooth path from GCSE to A-level history is a matter of building on and developing the basic understanding and skills already acquired.

This book offers the following signposts to assist that development. First, look for The Big Picture, and then identify the Key Issues. Next, locate sources of information, starting with the most accessible. On the way, take short-cuts to Enquiry and Investigation using Section 2. You will then reach the stage at which it is possible to form judgements, distil information and form coherent lines of argument. Finally, historians are judged on their ability to communicate.

Historical sources ?

'Probably the single most important development in twentieth-century historical studies is the broadening of our conception of what constitutes a historical source ...'
Arthur Marwick, The Nature of History (Macmillan, 3rd edn, 1989)

'Well I think it's been made perfectly clear that Jewish Italians have to decide whether they are Italians first or Jews. ... We must keep in step with our German comrades. Yes I know the Pope doesn't like it, but he has too much to lose to stick his neck out. He knows I can repeal the Lateran pacts. I've got a trident up his backside and he knows I can twist it.'
Mussolini speaking, page 10 of Louis de Bernières, Captain Corelli's Mandolin, 1994

Bearing in mind the above statement of Arthur Marwick, how would you judge if the 1994 novel, Captain Corelli's Mandolin, is of value as a historical source for the study of Fascist Italy?

Index